EFFECTIVE!
SEVEN KEYS FOR CHRISTIAN LEADERSHIP SUCCESS

DR. ARTHOR L. FABER

Arthor L. Faber Books

Effective! Seven Keys for Christian Leadership Success

Copyright 2025, by Arthor L. Faber

Requests for information should be addressed to:

Arthor L. Faber Books P.O. Box 165 Aquebogue NY 11931

ISBN 979-8-9987728-0-1 (Soft Cover)

ISBN 979-8-9987728-1-8 (E Book)

All scripture quotations and references, unless otherwise indicated, are taken from The Holy Bible, New International Version, NIV. Copyright 1973, 1978, 1984, 2011 by Biblica, Inc. All rights reserved to the owner of the publication.

All rights reserved.

No part of the publication may be reproduced, stored in a retrieval system, or transmitted in any form or by any means – electronic, mechanical, photocopy, recording, or any other, except for brief quotations in printed reviews, without the prior permission of the publisher.

Art direction: Abiodun T.
Interior design: Roberth Richard
Editing: Roberth Richard

DEDICATION

This writing is dedicated to:

Jesus Christ,

My Lord and Savior, whom I am inspired by

My Wife, Nicole, who is beyond what a supportive partner and loving friend should be.

And,

Oral Roberts University

My home away from home, and where God sent me many years ago, to find Him and experience him through many great scholars, professors, and lifelong friends who have changed my life.

God bless you all for being a testimony of God's faithfulness.

TABLE OF CONTENTS

The Calling (My Story) 1
Christian Leadership Defined (What is a Christian Leader) 4
Why Failure is Prevalent (Unpreparedness) 13
What's Necessary to Succeed as a Christian Leader (The 7 Keys) 19
Seven Questions to Advance Christian Leadership Understanding 25

Chapter one: The Key Chain 26
The Gift of the Holy Spirit 30
"WHO Is The Holy Spirit?" 32
Why the Holy Spirit is Important in Christian Leadership 35
The Holy Spirit Welcomed and Applied 38
Seven Questions to Advance a Leader's Understanding of the Holy Spirit 45
An Introduction to the Seven Keys 46

Chapter two: (Key One) Prayer 49
Prayer Life Defined 53
Daniel 57
Why Prayer is Important to Leadership 62
Prayer Application 64
Seven Questions to Advance the Understanding of Prayer for Christian Leadership Success 68

Chapter three: (Key Two) Faith 69

Faith Defined 73
Abraham 78
Why Faith is Important to Christian Leadership............ 80
Faith Applied 84
Seven Questions to Advance the Understanding of Faith for Christian Leadership Success 88

Chapter four: (Key Three) Integrity 89
Integrity Defined 91
Why Integrity is Imperative in Christian Leadership..... 93
Job... 94
Why Integrity is Important to Christian Leadership 97
Unapplied Integrity.. 101
Integrity Applied... 105
Seven Questions to Advance the Understanding of Integrity for Christian Leadership Success 107

Chapter five: (Key Four) Vision 108
Vision Defined.. 110
Peter 114
Why Vision is Important to Christian Leadership........ 116
Vision Applied.. 120
Seven Questions to Advance the Understanding of Vision for Christian Leadership Success 129

Chapter Six: (Key Five): Wisdom................................... 130
The Apostle Paul 139
Why Wisdom is Important to Christian Leadership..... 142
Wisdom Applied 145
Seven Questions to Advance the Understanding of Wisdom for Christian Leadership Success................... 148

Chapter Seven: (Key Six) Stewardship 149

    Stewardship Defined 151

    Joseph 155

    Why Stewardship is Important to the Christian Leader 158

    Stewardship Applied 161

    Stewardship Benefits: 161

    Seven Questions to Advance the Understanding of Stewardship for Christian Leadership Success 165

Chapter eight: (Key Seven): Agape Love 166

    Agape Love Defined 169

    The Good Samaritan 172

    Why Agape Love is Important to Christian Leadership 177

    Agape Love Applied 182

    Seven Questions to Advance the Understanding of Agape Love for Christian Leadership Success 186

the Conclusion 187

    A Hard Reset 190

    Christ: The Perfect Example 191

    Follow His Lead 192

    You Are Called to Be an Effective Christian Leader! .. 196

References 202

Biography 220

About The Author 221

Acknowledgements 223

THE CALLING (MY STORY)

"Son, I'm calling you to lead." Those six words were spoken to me more than fifteen years ago, yet I remember the moment as if it happened yesterday.

"You want me to lead? Lead what?" I thought. But deep down, I already knew who was speaking—and exactly what He was calling me to lead.

By then, I had been circling around the church for years—over a decade, in fact. Even as a child, I could sense that the Church of Jesus Christ, and being a part of its core leadership, was something I was meant for. And if I'm being honest, a part of me *wanted* it. But like so many others, I wrestled with the feeling of being unprepared and unqualified. That's where the struggle begins for many of us—not with the calling itself, but with whether we believe we're worthy of it.

"Who was I?" I thought aloud when the challenge—how I saw it—was placed before me. "Who would listen to me?" What could I say or do that would inspire people not only to follow me as I followed God?" These thoughts, and many more, were meant to discourage me from answering God's call. They served as reasons for me to continue resisting Him and refuse His guidance in becoming who He had destined me to be. My reasoning for declining began with the absence of pastoral mentorship or clear examples of what the role of a pastor truly entailed—correct behaviors, practices, and

duties. For me, the easiest escape was to disqualify myself, from ignoring God's calling because I feared directly saying no.

As most would probably assume, this tactic of denying God's command failed miserably. It took me two years to wave the white flag and submit to God's will. I believe this was an essential part of the process. Many people, when sharing their ministry experiences with me, reflect on God's call and their immediate response to denial. While I don't dismiss that experience, it was not mine. Once I agreed to follow, I began to see how God was slowly shifting every aspect of my being to prepare me for the transformation required for Christian leadership. Much of this I couldn't recognize at the moment, but as I continued to move forward, I began to see the changes unfold in real time. Maturity started to take root, and confidence—though still growing—began to emerge within me. Overall, I knew I wasn't alone in this journey. It became clear that God wasn't just walking beside me; He was leading the way.

It was clear that I was becoming the person I was meant to be. Like many other leaders, this moment was both defining and spiritually affirming. I resonated deeply with the statement, "You are where you should be, and you are becoming the person God designed you to be." For me, this was an incredible realization.

However, there is a reality that lies beyond that moment. The truth is, that leadership—regardless of its form—is about helping others become who they are meant to be. That led me to a question I began to ask myself: *How?* How do I lead? How do I play this vital role in the lives of those God would position to walk alongside me?

Once again, I found myself facing uncertainty—not because the task seemed insurmountable, but because I was anxious. I feared disappointing God.

I believed that God believed in me, and I didn't want to disappoint Him. That fear of failure was something I saw all too often in the lives of leaders around me. Over the years, I witnessed many resign due to burnout, quit because of mental anguish, or get removed because of irresponsible behavior. Some crumbled internally because they lacked what was needed to perform the calling they had been given.

On the other hand, I knew leaders who worked tirelessly, devoted themselves to helping people, and invested in their church organizations. Yet, to them, their labor seemed to amount to very little. To outsiders, they were often viewed as failures—just like those I had mentioned earlier.

As a maturing believer in Christ who believed, "I can do all things," I found myself asking, in the midst of all the failure around me, *What do I need to possess for my leadership calling to be successful?*

The topic of failure is not an easy one to discuss. For current leaders, there's little opportunity to invite future colleagues to learn how to avoid failure. Failure is often seen through a negative lens, and because we avoid talking about it, we assume we can prevent it. Yet, if we're honest, we all know that's far from the truth. Failure is something that many, if not all, people experience in some form at some point in life.

The key questions about failure are: First, if one experiences it, did they make failure valuable? What did they learn from it, and is that lesson worth documenting? Second, can the lesson from failure be shared in a way that helps others avoid the same mistake? More specifically, what can a Christian leader do or obtain to prevent failure in their role?

I believe that not just the failures themselves, but the lessons learned from them, can be converted into "key" principles and attributes that are valuable to both current leaders and those like me, who are concerned about possessing what's necessary for success in leadership. This writing aims to share these lessons, emphasizing seven specific characteristics, principles, and attributes that a leader should cultivate. By incorporating these into their leadership approach, they can divert failure and better prepare themselves for the many challenges ahead.

CHRISTIAN LEADERSHIP DEFINED (WHAT IS A CHRISTIAN LEADER)

The Christian leader we see today is, unfortunately, often undervalued. The role is frequently misunderstood, and as a result, the identity and purpose of a Christian leader are often misconstrued. A Christian leader is not just a preacher, a counselor, or someone to turn to when strife arrives. They are not only the one who prays for you. The Christian leader must be much more than that, because—though the world may not always recognize it—this calling demands more.

To truly understand the Christian leader, we must first define what Christian leadership is.

Defining Christian leadership is a process. While it is often seen as complex, Christian leadership becomes easier to understand once we first establish what leadership itself entails. Leadership development expert J. Robert Clinton offers a helpful definition, describing leadership as a dynamic process over an extended period, in which a positioned overseer influences the thoughts and activities of followers to accomplish goals that benefit not only the leader but also the followers and the larger context they are part of (Clinton, 2012).

Peter Northouse, a widely recognized authority on the subject, defines leadership as a process in which an individual influences a group of people to achieve a specific goal.

Leadership involves influence, particularly in how leaders affect followers and establish communication between them. Leaders form relationships with their followers, create links of communication, and bear the responsibility of maintaining those relationships (Northouse, 2022). Northouse's understanding of leadership naturally aligns with the concept of servant leadership, which further shapes our understanding of the Christian leader.

Robert Greenleaf, the renowned author of *Servant Leadership*, defines a servant leader as someone who embodies the mind and heart of a "servant first." Through this mindset of servitude, the individual is drawn into the role of leadership. The servant leader prioritizes the needs of others, ensuring that the highest needs of those they lead are met.

The impact of servant leadership is twofold: the leader grows as an individual through their servitude, and so do those they serve. Those recognizing the leader's role in servitude also experience personal growth, becoming healthier, wiser, more accessible, more autonomous, and more likely to embrace the role of servant leader themselves (Greenleaf, 2002).

Northouse further supports the premise of servant leadership, emphasizing the development of followers through assertive moral behavior toward them, the organization, and the stakeholders they represent. To be effective, servant leadership involves several key characteristics: listening, empathy, healing, awareness, persuasion, conceptualization, foresight, responsibility, trustworthiness, commitment to the growth of people, and the building of community (Northouse, 2022).

With a clearer understanding of leadership and servitude— both essential for the role of a Christian overseer—we can better define Christian leadership. Aubrey Malphurs offers one of the most profound views of Christian leadership, describing Christian leaders as servants with the credibility and capabilities to influence people within a given context, guiding them to pursue their God-given direction. Since Christian leadership is a calling, leaders are expected to lead in any context, whether within or outside their Christian community or organization (Malphurs, 2003).

Christian leadership, at its core, is about influencing and serving others in alignment with Christ's interests, all while fulfilling God's purposes through them. Within this role, the leader, by living out and sharing the truth of the gospel, helps those they lead to live holy lives that please God. A Christian leader, as a steward of God's Kingdom, demonstrates the character of Jesus Christ to the world (Omoasegun, 2022).

Christian leadership begins with God and finds its foundation in the life and teachings of Jesus Christ. The leader, as God's distinctive presence and revelation in human history, must prioritize God's will and, despite the frustrations of a broken world, live it out with humility and wisdom. These attributes are visually reflected in a true Christian leader (Sloan, 2010).

Christian leadership requires not only an empowering mentality but also good character. Leaders must understand their responsibility, which encompasses significant power and authority. These privileges must be viewed as gifts from God, aligning with the leader's desire to see the church grow and flourish, ultimately bringing glory to God and equipping the church (Buckland, 2012). This distinction between Christian leadership and secular leadership becomes clear in these aspects.

A leader who lives by faith in Jesus Christ has a purpose that extends beyond ordinary leadership principles such as communication, judgment, and integrity. The purpose of Christian leadership is to glorify God by guiding others to grow in faith and service to Him (Barton, 2022). Faith cannot be separated from leadership; rather, one's devotion to Christ enhances and strengthens leadership, creating more opportunities to meaningfully impact others (Leadership Ministries, 2023).

The final critical element that defines Christian leadership is the leader's ability to focus on the future. This involves assessing current changes that may provide a glimpse into the future and leading accordingly toward what is projected. Termed future-focused leadership, this essential behavior requires leaders and their teams to think differently about today, about change, about tomorrow, and about the future of leadership (Petty & Vande Zane, 2022).

Being future-focused is closely associated with a leader's vision—the crucial ability to guide organizations and groups through a well-established plan toward an envisioned goal.

While the leader may assess the path forward, the goal itself is ultimately established by God.

Building on the insights presented in these writings, I now offer the following definition of Christian leadership, which will guide this discussion. Christian leadership is the role of a spiritually called, Christ-devoted, sacrificial servant who adheres to and implements biblical standards. The leader guides individuals to live Christ-centered lives, achieve both current and future goals, and continually strengthen their faith. Furthermore, a Christian leader influences others by encouraging them to draw closer to God and respond effectively to their own leadership calling (Malphurs, 2016).

This definition became personally significant when I sensed God calling me into Christian leadership. Initially, I struggled to grasp what it truly meant. Like many, I equated Christian leadership with being a pastor or holding a position within the church. While that was indeed my path, I began to recognize that the modern-day image of church leaders doesn't always reflect the full scope of what a Christian leader is called to be. This realization highlighted the importance of having a clear, biblically grounded definition to guide both understanding and practice.

It is God's will that Christian leaders are present in His churches, Christian-based organizations, and throughout society. The role of a "Christian leader" is sacred, not only to churches and Christian organizations, but also to the broader mission of advancing God's Kingdom (Costello, 2023). Through these called individuals, God's work is carried out, and the faith is furthered. Christian leaders are at the forefront of shaping the lives of God's people, enabling them to find stability and, eventually, flourish in their faith.

This approach to leadership, established by Jesus Christ and further structured by the Apostles, has been passed down through the centuries. The leadership principles first implemented by early Christian leaders continue to influence and guide Christian leaders today, contributing to the ongoing success of Christian leadership throughout history.

One thing must be clear about Christian leaders: they are not simply leaders who happen to be Christians—they are Christians first, who lead because they are called to do so. Their identity in Christ precedes their leadership.

These individuals did not step into leadership as a career choice, nor did they earn their roles through courses, certifications, or occupational merit. Christian leaders are appointed through a divine calling from God (Larson, 2017). Because of this calling, their primary objective is to satisfy and glorify God through their leadership.

When God is placed first in every area of their life—including their leadership—His guidance becomes evident. As Matthew 6:33 (NIV) reminds us, "But seek first his kingdom and his righteousness, and all these things will be given to you as well." In doing so, the Christian leaders' journey unfolds in unexpected, fruitful ways— often beyond their own expectations—and becomes a testimony of effective, Spirit-led leadership.

This underscores why understanding the definition of Christian leadership is so important. Christian leaders are called to be examples. They are to demonstrate and reflect who Christ is, and to embody what a follower of Christ can—and should—become.

Beyond setting an example, they are also protectors, teachers, and correctors of the flock. Even in times of difficulty or danger, their public obedience to Christ becomes a testimony—one that inspires those following them to see Jesus through their actions.

A Christian leader must never forget the image they bear. It is the image and identity of the One who called them, and it is that reflection of Christ they are entrusted to show to the world.

Today, the visible image of the Christian leader is not always what it should be. Sadly, there has been a noticeable compromise concerning the integrity of the role (Piper, 2024). Whether in church settings or professional environments, it seems that everyone claims to be a Christian—and many assert that their leadership calling, position, and influence are endorsed by Christ.

However, if someone seeking Christ were to observe many of today's so-called Christian leaders, they might be met with confusion, or worse, disillusionment. They would likely see inconsistency, even hypocrisy. And like I once did, they could walk away unsure, disheartened, or completely disinterested.

The statistics only deepen the concern. According to Gallup's 2023 Honesty and Ethics poll, public trust in clergy declined for the fourth consecutive year, dropping to 32%—down from 34% the year before. This marks the first time in Gallup's history that fewer than one-third of Americans believe pastors possess high or very high levels of honesty and ethics (Earls, 2024a).

Why does such a statistic exist? Because the failure rate among Christian leaders of all kinds continues to rise. In the United States, more than 1,500 pastors leave the ministry each month due to moral failure, spiritual burnout, or poor leadership practices (Barton, 2022).

Lifeway reported that in 2015, pastors were stepping away from the pulpit at an annual rate of 1.3%. By 2021, that number had increased to 1.5%—a troubling trend that shows no signs of reversing.

The same study also found that pastors increasingly feel overwhelmed in their roles. In 2015, 54% of pastors reported feeling frequently overwhelmed. By 2021, that number had risen to 63% (Earls, 2024b).

Similar leadership struggles are occurring globally. In Nigeria, for example, churches are experiencing high levels of pastoral departures—both voluntary and involuntary. These exits are often linked to government interference, where efforts to influence church leadership have compromised the authenticity of many leaders' callings.

Corruption is also a persistent issue. In some cases, funds from tithes, offerings, and other church-generated income are misappropriated, ending up in the private accounts of administrators. Poor leadership skills among church leaders have further hindered effective church management. The lack of training and development exposes pastors to administrative challenges that impact the stewardship of resources.

These issues often lead to problems such as embezzlement, stagnation in ministry growth, and the mass departure of congregants. Ultimately, such failures can result in the removal of pastors and leaders from their positions (Jegede, 2023).

In South Korea, where Christianity was once considered to be experiencing " a religious explosion," growth has now slowed to a crawl. The Center for the Study of Global Christianity estimates that from 2000 to 2020, the Christian population will have increased from 31% to only 33%. It is then projected to stay at that level through 2050. Zylstra attributes this stagnation to the public failures of church leadership—failures that were initially overlooked but have become impossible to deny given the enormity of the congregations involved.

One pastor was jailed for raping eight female followers, claiming it was "on orders from God." Another was convicted of embezzling $12 million. Yet another leader was publicly criticized for attempting to pass his church of 100,000 members on to his son (Zylstra, 2019).

These are not isolated incidents. From regional to national levels, the reports of leadership failure within the Christian community are undeniable. It is a global issue, and it's everywhere around us. And as someone who is called the lead, I unfortunately witness many of my colleagues departing their roles and, for one of the reasons just described, concluding their leadership engagements as a failure, and how easily it could happen if I was not vigilant.

The purpose of highlighting these examples of Christian leadership failure is to illustrate how daunting this position was for me—and continues to be for others—despite it being a divine calling from God. Many devoted Christians and leaders, like myself, often ask, "Will my leadership experience end in this way?"

The answer is not simply about the failure of leadership itself. We must seek to understand the root causes of these failures to truly grasp why they happen. If many are called, what is going wrong for so many that leads to failure? And, perhaps even more crucial, what can we do to prevent these failures from happening repeatedly?

WHY FAILURE IS PREVALENT (UNPREPAREDNESS)

Whether we fully realize it or not, Adam was the first to be called to lead. God gave him dominion over all creation and entrusted him with the responsibility to honor Him by stewarding everything placed in his care. In this, Adam was set apart as the original model for leadership.

When God blessed Adam with Eve, the divine framework for leadership began to take shape: the man was to lead the woman, and God was to lead the man. If this order remained intact, blessings would flow, and God's blessing would rest upon His creation.

Unfortunately, the story did not unfold as hoped. The breakdown of that original leadership structure is one we still experience today.

What appeared to be Adam's unpreparedness—or perhaps his passivity—opened the door for Satan. The enemy deceived Eve into disregarding God's word, while Adam stood by, silently observing, saying, and doing nothing.

The consequence of this failure was severe. Adam lost his position, was removed from the Garden, and his leadership tenure came to be remembered as a failure—one rooted not in a lack of calling, but in the failure to fulfill it.

We must understand that God gave Adam everything he needed. But having the tools is not the same as knowing how to use them. Access does not automatically translate to understanding or effective application.

This remains true for leaders today. Many find themselves in turmoil, overwhelmed in their roles, unsure of how they ended up in such chaos. When asked what led to their breaking point or why a particular challenge overcame them, their answers—often shared after seasons of prayer and reflection—are strikingly similar: *"I wasn't prepared."* They had read about such moments. They had seen them unfold in the lives of others. Through education and training, they had been exposed to the possibilities. But when the moment came, they found themselves unready—not because they lacked knowledge, but because they lacked preparation at the heart and soul level.

But when it finally happened—when the moment came to define their role—many leaders, though equipped with resources and knowledge, found themselves unable to respond effectively. They had what they needed, but didn't fully understand how to utilize what they possessed. And in that crucial moment, they mishandled the opportunity—*they dropped the ball.*

Some, like Adam, didn't know how to properly use what had been given to them. To illustrate this, consider a chef working in a kitchen. They understand the power and purpose of fire—it's essential to their craft. They use it to cook, to bring ingredients to life. But sometimes, though rarely, that same fire can spiral out of control, leading to chaos or even an emergency.

That's why most chefs are trained in fire prevention. They know about fire blankets, baking soda, and the trusty fire extinguisher. They've been taught what to do in the event of a fire.

But what happens if, in the panic of the moment, the chef freezes? What if they can't recall the right steps? What if the fire extinguisher isn't nearby or is forgotten altogether? Some might say, "They should've made sure everything was in place before they started cooking." But in truth, many don't—because the possibility of fire seems unlikely.

This is exactly how it is for many Christian leaders. The idea of facing a challenge so severe it could cause them to fail seems far-fetched—until it isn't. The truth is, like Adam, failure happens. And it happens when we are unprepared, when we don't truly understand what we possess, or how to properly use what God has already placed in our hands.

What comes the way of a Christian leader? Ultimately, all leaders face leadership fatigue—burnout—and are presented with invitations to yield to temptation (Winston & Patterson, 2006). When a leader's internal strength and spiritual discipline are lacking, it often culminates in the kind of failure the Christian world has, unfortunately, grown far too accustomed to witnessing.

So, the question we must now ask is: *What exactly are Christian leaders—whether leading churches or organizations—so often unprepared for?*

The answer lies in the kinds of challenges that don't just disrupt a leader—they derail them. These are the moments that result in resignation, dismissal, or quiet departures. And they're more common than many realize.

A five-year survey conducted by Barna reveals eye-opening trends among pastors across the United States. Many reported feeling ill-equipped to meet the core demands of leadership— pointing to significant gaps in their training.

For instance, in 2015, only 27% of pastors said they wished they had been better prepared to handle conflict. By 2020, that number rose sharply to 40%. In 2015, 20% of pastors wished they were better equipped to delegate and train others—by 2020, that number had more than doubled to 41%. Likewise, in 2015, just 16% wished for better preparation in navigating church politics. But by 2020, 36% acknowledged it as a critical shortfall (Kinnaman, 2023; Latchaw, 2023).

The data also highlights a generational gap. Younger pastors—those under 45—reported higher levels of unpreparedness in nearly every area compared to their older counterparts. For example, 47% of younger pastors felt unprepared to handle conflict versus 37% of pastors over 45. When it came to crisis management, 32% of younger pastors reported a lack of preparation, compared to just 15% of older pastors. Leadership demands? 29% versus 17% (Kinnaman, 2023).

Additionally, another Barna report revealed which areas leaders themselves identified as underdeveloped or missing entirely in their training. These include courage (27%), discipline (17%), vision (15%), and a deep, enduring passion for God (13%) (Lomenick, 2013).

These numbers expose a significant concern: many Christian leaders are stepping into roles without the tools, techniques, or support systems needed to thrive. Over the last two to three decades, this lack of preparation has contributed to an alarming rise in leadership failures across ministries.

This pervasive sense of unpreparedness cultivates a deeper, more personal reality: leader discouragement. Leaders begin to experience a lack of fulfillment in their roles. They question their effectiveness, their qualifications, and ultimately, their calling. This internal struggle often marks the early stages of personal breakdown, flawed decision-making, and evidence of immature leadership development (Magnelli, 2020).

Strategist Jeremy Latchaw captures the gravity of this phase: "80% of pastors reported feeling unqualified or ineffective in their current role, and 30% said they were *very* unqualified or ineffective. Additionally, 40% of pastors said they were struggling with discouragement due to the demands and expectations placed on them" (Latchaw, 2023).

These numbers tell a painful truth: a significant portion of Christian leaders feel overwhelmed, under-equipped, and disheartened. This emotional and spiritual fatigue leads to diminished job satisfaction, higher burnout rates, and, ultimately, early departures from ministry.

Even more troubling is the lack of perceived support. Many leaders actively seek help, mentorship, or simply someone to confide in—but don't believe such assistance is available. Whether due to a lack of communication, fear of judgment, or systemic issues within denominations, many do not realize that support is both available and, in some denominations, actively provided (Costello, 2017).

A staggering 65% of pastors report having little or no access to leadership training or resources. Over half (54%) say they receive minimal or no support from their church leadership team (Latchaw, 2023). This "left-out-to-dry" feeling only amplifies the weight of their responsibilities.

The outcome? Leaders flatline. Many spirals into discouragement, moral or ethical compromise, or emotional and mental deterioration. For some, it ends with forced resignation. For others, it's a silent collapse—still showing up, but barely holding on.

Surveys, testimonial reports, and much of the existing literature make one truth increasingly clear: the ill-preparedness of leaders significantly hinder their ability to overcome the challenges they face.

Yet, if God has called a leader, then that leader—through the empowerment of the Holy Spirit—possesses everything necessary to become the person God has designated them to be. What the leader may lack in the moment, God will provide. That provision is not in question.

The more pressing issue is this: many leaders do not struggle from *lack of access* to tools, principles, or spiritual attributes. Instead, they struggle with a lack of understanding—of what these tools are, why they are essential, and how to use them effectively.

This writing exists to present, illuminate, and thoroughly explain what God has made available. It aims to reveal what leaders need to understand, embrace, and implement to overcome the inevitable challenges of leadership, thrive in their calling, and become the effective, faithful leaders God has created and commissioned them to be.

What's Necessary to Succeed as a Christian Leader (The 7 Keys)

For many leaders, something is missing. But it's not that they don't *have* it—it's that they're not *using* it. Some are using God-given tools, gifts, and attributes—but not always, not consistently, not correctly, and not when they are needed most.

Take, for example, wisdom—one of the most sacred and essential attributes that God offers. Wisdom is critical to Christian leadership because it directly influences decision-making, discernment, and the ability to navigate complex choices and challenges. Yet many leaders either misuse it, ignore it, or treat it as optional—something to shelve until the crisis hits—rather than living by it as God intended.

When leaders don't use wisdom *thoroughly*—when it's misapplied, overlooked, or disregarded—they contradict God's very purpose in providing it (Karthikeyan, 2024). And when Christians reflect on the challenges of handling wisdom well, one biblical figure immediately comes to mind: Solomon.

Solomon became king of Israel after inheriting the throne from his father, David. Once established, he sought the Lord—and God, pleased with his heart, offered Solomon the opportunity to ask for anything he desired. Solomon, humbly aware of his own inadequacy, asked for wisdom—recognizing that it was essential to rule God's people with justice and discernment.

God honored his request and granted Solomon wisdom, along with wealth and prosperity beyond what any king before or after him would experience. His wisdom was evident early in his reign. One notable example is the well-known dispute between two women, each claiming to be the mother of the same child. Solomon's handling of the situation stunned the people of Israel and affirmed that God's wisdom was with him.

His wisdom continued to shine as he answered every question presented by the Queen of Sheba—so thoroughly that she marveled at his insight, declaring that nothing was too difficult for the king to explain. Solomon also wisely and faithfully completed the construction of the Temple in Jerusalem, a project initiated by his father but entrusted to him for completion.

But as his reign progressed, the cracks began to show. The very wisdom that had made him great seemed to fade from use in his personal life—where temptation, compromise, and disobedience entered. Though he had received wisdom from God, Solomon did not always apply it in the areas that mattered most. This marked the beginning of his decline and exposed a critical truth: having wisdom is not the same as using it consistently and faithfully.

God had a directive concerning the Israelites, one that Solomon was seemingly knowledgeable of, and it concerned his adoration for women.

King Solomon, however, loved many foreign women besides Pharaoh's daughter—Moabites, Ammonites, Edomites, Sidonians, and Hittites. (2) They were from nations about which the Lord had told the Israelites, "You must not intermarry with them because they will surely turn your hearts after their gods." Nevertheless, Solomon held fast to them in love. (3) He had seven hundred wives of royal birth and three hundred concubines, and his wives led him astray. (1 King 11:1-3, NIV)

Despite the wisdom he possessed, Solomon disobeyed God when it came to marriage. While he was wise in certain aspects of his rulership, he faltered in matters concerning himself. As the scripture reveals, his failure—or perhaps unwillingness—to apply wisdom in this area led him to marry foreign women. These marriages would ultimately influence his persistent disobedience toward God, escalating into further acts of rebellion. This, in turn, culminated in an internal conflict that divided Israel into two separate kingdoms. While Solomon's reign included many successes, this disobedience cast a shadow over his leadership, highlighting it as an overall failure (Menking, 2017).

Unfortunately, many leaders have failed to learn from Solomon's mistake or believe that such failures could never happen during their own leadership. Yet, for many, they do. Solomon's downfall occurred because he misused or neglected to utilize the wisdom that God had granted him for such a crucial moment. The Bible illustrates how Solomon's actions led to his flawed leadership, and this parallels how many Christian leaders, over time, see their influence and role as a guiding voice end in organizational destruction and failure.

Solomon held the role of king and had access to many of the tools (attributes) essential for ruling effectively. However, because he seemed unaware of their purpose or how to use them properly, his reign, though meaningful, didn't fulfill the expectations he or others (according to Ecclesiastes) had for it. This challenge is one that many Christian leaders face today. Many leaders within the

Christian church and organizations are currently grappling with the typical stressors and challenges of leadership (Sloan, 2010). These pressures often distract Christian leaders, causing them to lose focus and, unfortunately, steer themselves and the organizations they lead in the wrong direction—resulting in a negative outcome (Malphurs, 2023). This frequently leads to organizational breakdown and dysfunction, prompting leaders to leave, whether voluntarily or through force (Graham, 2020b). However, what we often see is that these same leaders face similar hardships but fail to use the God-given attributes, principles, and tools—the necessary "keys"— that could help them navigate through the struggles and maintain headship, even when it seems impossible (Huizing, 2011).

Failure in Christian leadership, as many have witnessed, is avoidable, and it is crucial that it be prevented at all costs. The harm caused by such failure is not always felt immediately, but it eventually surfaces and has a lasting impact on those who are following the leader's example in faith. Jim and Tammy Bakker are unfortunate examples of this. Their world-renowned ministry in the 1970s and 1980s touched many lives, revealing Christ to countless congregants and television viewers. However, when a scandal involving sexual immorality and financial misconduct came to light, not only did their ministry collapse, but their personal lives unraveled as well, leading to divorce, imprisonment, and further troubling revelations. Additionally, their failures tainted many people's faith in the Christian church. Many who trusted these leaders became disillusioned—not just with the church, but with their belief in Jesus Christ (Effron, 2019). While faithful believers should never place their trust in man over Christ, many followers develop a deep devotion to their leaders. They look to them not only for spiritual guidance but also to see what a life with Christ truly looks like. When a leader's Christian Walk is revealed to be fraudulent, many become discouraged, feeling that if their leader can't make it, neither can they (Malphurs, 2003). This is why Christian leadership, in any capacity, is of utmost importance. It is a delicate subject that must be approached with the utmost seriousness, especially by those called to the role. God knew leadership for us would be challenging.

This becomes evident when we review the ministry of Jesus. Jesus was not only the high priest to all humanity, but also the leader of twelve men whom He was preparing for the greatest mission ever: to spread His message of love, mercy, and grace to the world. What a daunting task for our Lord, yet one that was essential for His special gift to be shared and received by all. Jesus was the first to exemplify the very principles this writing emphasizes. God the Father equipped Him with specific characteristics, principles, tools, and traits to overcome the challenges He would face—challenges that could have derailed Him from His mission (Barton, 2022). However, because our Lord effectively used these "keys," His mission was accomplished, and we exist as Christians today because He did not fail in His ministry (Kimball, 1977). While we are obviously not Christ and are far from perfect, as individuals called to follow Him, we must utilize what He has shared with us to fulfill the calling He has placed in our hearts. This writing highlights these "keys" that we saw in Christ—and if we're honest, we must recognize them in ourselves as leaders.

When I first entered the field of Christian leadership many years ago, I was given a metaphorical "keychain" with many keys— tools designed to help me lead in ways that would not only solidify my position but also fulfill the true calling of a leader: to guide those entrusted to my care, pointing them in the right direction toward the Lord by allowing them to witness a life fully submitted to Christ. The challenge I faced from the beginning was that, despite having a set of "keys," I didn't yet understand their value, purpose, or how to use them correctly to be the leader both I and those I was meant to lead needed me to be. This writing serves two purposes: first, as an offering to those entering leadership, and second, as a reminder for current leaders in the Christian faith of what we already possess. This book will clearly define each "key," offer a Biblical example demonstrating its use by our forefathers and explain its God-given purpose. Additionally, I will explain why these "keys" are crucial and when they should be used. There will be seven in total, as seven signifies completion, and our goal is to become complete leaders— fully prepared for the tasks before us. By implementing these keys, as Christ did, we aim not only for success but for effectiveness in our roles as Christian leaders.

Seven Questions to Advance Christian Leadership Understanding

1. How would you define an effective leader?

2. How important is sufficient education and training toward a leader's effectiveness?

3. What qualities do you believe an effective leader should possess for success?

4. What are some detriments that you believe provoke Christian leadership failure?

5. In your opinion, what would disqualify an individual from being an effective Christian leader?

6. If you were called to be a Christian leader, what would be the most important possession that you believe would assist you in being an effective leader?

7. How important is mentorship when it comes to developing new leaders?

Chapter One
The Key Chain

I was a church kid, though I realize that phrase might mean different things to different people. For me, it means I grew up in the church, and the formation of my identity today is deeply rooted in the Christian faith. I don't have the story some might share, where every moment of my life was spent in church. However, I did spend a lot of time there, and the church became a natural part of what I considered to be a fulfilling life. Because my family was deeply involved in the church and I loved being immersed in family life, when people asked what I had done earlier, where I was the day before, or what my plans were for the weekend, my response often involved being at church.

Church life in the late 1970s and early 1980s, in my opinion, was different from what it is today. Perhaps I reminisce on the time the way I do because I was a child at the time. Though I was a child, I was highly influenced by adults, with May being around a majority of the time. Some would later become mentors and influencers in my life. Many of them were family, and some, though not blood relatives, felt just like family. They all showed me how God was working through them in various ways, shaping who I would become as I grew older. One of these influential figures was my "Uncle Frank." Frank was my grandmother's sister's husband's brother (not a blood relative), but he took me under his wing, letting me follow him as he carried out his duties as the custodian at our large church.

Uncle Frank amazed me in many ways. First, he seemed to do everything. While I might be exaggerating to some, from my perspective, he was often called upon, and when he was, he always delivered. Through Frank, I was also introduced to the values of reliability and integrity. On many occasions, I saw him provide for others when the odds seemed impossible, all while honoring his word and staying faithful to what was right. The impressionable lesson I learned from Frank, though, came from something he allowed me to witness, though I don't think he realized how significant it was for me. Uncle Frank had access, mainly because of the role he played at the church. Because of this access, Uncle Frank could unlock doors that led to other doors, which in turn opened up rooms and areas that were beneficial to those who needed what those rooms contained. It wasn't that these rooms were off-limits to others.

Rather, to enter them and use what they offered, you needed access.

And access was only available to the one who had the "key" to unlock the door.

I remember it like it was yesterday. Watching Uncle Frank access his keychain, a large set of keys attached to his belt, hung on his right hip. With a simple pull, he would extend the keychain to the lock that needed to be opened. The keychain held several clearly labeled keys, each one meant to unlock doors to rooms that people needed access to. I recall times when someone would request access to a specific room, and I would follow Uncle Frank as he unlocked one door after another. What struck me during these moments was how each key played a crucial role. As he went from door to door, using each key to unlock them, he would carefully note their markings, understanding exactly which key granted access to what was needed by those who sought to utilize the room's resources.

One day, Uncle Frank caught me staring at his keychain— he clearly knew how fascinated I was by them— and decided to explain something important about the keys. He said, "Art, I can see you understand the importance of the keys, but do you know what's just as important as the keys themselves?" Naturally, I didn't have an answer. He went on to explain that the "keychain" is just as, if not more, important than the keys. He made it clear that the keychain keeps the keys together in a specific sequence, allowing them to be used effectively, easily identified for efficiency, and secured so they don't get lost. When the time comes to use them, they must be easily accessible. Without the keychain, he explained, access would be limited, and proper use would be jeopardized. That made me realize how easy it would be to be denied access at a crucial moment—the exact moment when that key could make the difference between success and failure—if we mishandled or lost a specific key.

Have you ever experienced something in your youth that you knew was significant, but at the time, you didn't fully understand its meaning or why it was something you needed to remember? My time with Uncle Frank was just that. When I began my first role in Christian leadership, I was introduced by many honorable and distinguished Christian leaders to attributes, principles, and tools that would shape the kind of leader I would become. These gifts would contribute to the effectiveness of my calling. However, though I possessed these attributes, principles, and tools, they weren't properly organized. Because they lacked structure, they became disordered and ineffective, leading to early leadership approaches that fell short. In many ways, I moved forward in doubt, despite having these unique gifts. The truth was, I didn't yet understand how these attributes, principles, and tools would function together with proper use or how to use them effectively.

In contrast, when used correctly, each of these attributes, principles, and tools should complement one another, culminating in an outcome far beyond what I could have imagined, especially considering my inexperience. As I reflected on my time with Uncle Frank, I realized that there were many locks (opportunities) before me, but only the use of the correct key would give me access, allowing success to follow. However, because of my lack of confidence and unpreparedness regarding leadership, I believed that I didn't have what I needed to possess, when I fact, I was fully equipped. What I was doing in ignorance was attempting to use the wrong key to unlock the doors before me to gain access.

Through this setback, I gained clarity on an important lesson—one that became clear after understanding what God was doing through my experience with Uncle Frank. Uncle Frank had access to many essential resources, but it took his keys to unlock them. However, the keys needed to be properly identified, organized, and secured to be used effectively. In the same way, God gives every leader attributes, principles, and tools to be effective in their calling. A significant issue many leaders face is improperly identifying these attributes, principles, and tools. We often fail to organize them properly, and as a result, we aren't fully secure in their proper use. So the question became: What allows these God-given attributes, principles, and tools to be used effectively? Just like Uncle Frank, who was only able to use his keys effectively because they were secured on a strong keychain, we as leaders must properly use the "keychain" the Lord has given us. That keychain is the Holy Spirit, who enables us to identify, organize, and use the keys God has entrusted to us.

THE GIFT OF THE HOLY SPIRIT

Every Christian leader who has faith in Jesus Christ possesses the gift of the Holy Spirit. I am confident in this because of the promises Jesus made. To be clear, the Holy Spirit, as our advocate (John 14:26), is not just for leaders but for all believers (Finney, 1980). However, for leaders, if we allow the Holy Spirit to take control of who we are and the work we've been called to lead and influence, then our success as leaders isn't based solely on our human gifts, but on the power the Holy Spirit provides. God, through His Spirit, molds and shapes all believers, including leaders, in ways that enable them to become all they are meant to be. The Spirit, at God's direction, forms leaders, defines their identity, and determines their calling or purpose in the Kingdom (Thomson, 2017).

Reflecting on the Old Testament, the prophet Jeremiah observed a potter at work, shaping clay into the vessel that was desired or required (Jer. 11:2-4, NIV). In the same way, God designs leaders, shaping and forming them through a process guided and ordained by the Holy Spirit (Thomson, 2017).

This truth is made clear biblically on many occasions. When the disciples took up the ministry after Jesus' ascension, as recorded in the book of Acts, He told them, "You will receive power when the Holy Spirit has come upon you, and you will be my witnesses in Jerusalem and in all Judea and Samaria, and to the end of the earth" (Acts 1:8, NIV). The Apostle Paul, after his transformative encounter with Jesus on the road to Damascus, was led to meet a devout believer named Ananias. When they met, Ananias said, "Saul, my brother, the Lord Jesus has sent me to pray for you so that you might see again and be filled with the Holy Spirit" (Acts 9:17, NIV). Finally, to highlight the most important example, we cannot leave Jesus out of this discussion. At Jesus' baptism, "Heaven was opened, and he saw the Spirit of God descending like a dove and alighting on him" (Matt. 3:16, NIV).

With the understanding of Jesus' call for the Christian faith to spread throughout the world, and referencing the three leaders mentioned above, it is clear that God provided each of them with unique attributes, principles, and tools to fulfill their calling as leaders. Although divine, Jesus Himself also relied on the Holy Spirit, choosing not to enter humanity, history, and ministry alone, but with the continual presence of the Spirit (Cross, 2007). The Holy Spirit served as the connector between the divine and human in Jesus. In this way, Christ demonstrated to His followers what the Holy Spirit could and would do for those who placed their faith in Him, just as the Spirit guided countless Biblical heroes and modern-day Christ-followers toward the success God had positioned them to achieve.

What is clear is that, despite all they possessed, it was the power of the Holy Spirit that kept everything in order, in mind, and accessible. It was the Holy Spirit that allowed the gifts they received to be used effectively. The success they experienced in utilizing what God gave them to impact the world was rooted in their understanding of who the Holy Spirit is and how He elevates the use of God's "keys" to a level far beyond our ability to comprehend. But this can be achieved when every key is connected to our God-given keychain—the Holy Spirit.

"WHO IS THE HOLY SPIRIT?"

Note that the statement above does not attempt to explain what the Holy Spirit is, because the Holy Spirit is not an "it," but a person. C.S. Lewis once shared that, though people may know God, they often know Him only vaguely. However, when Jesus entered the world, He provided an image of God that allowed the world to truly believe in Him. After His death, resurrection, and ascension, the movement of faith began, and those leading it found God within themselves. It was the Holy Spirit who directed these believers and empowered them to accomplish things they would not have been able to do on their own (Lewis, 1980).

This is where the true power lies for Christians. The Holy Spirit, one of the three persons of the Godhead, is the gift that equips us. As Dr. Billy Graham stated, the Holy Spirit is the "source of power who meets our need to escape the miserable weakness that often grips us" (1988a). The Spirit empowers us to be who God has called us to be. In this context, the Holy Spirit enables us to become the leaders that God has ordained us to be. But this leads to the crucial question: "Who is the Holy Spirit?"

It is essential to first understand that the Holy Spirit is God. This is evident through His attributes. The Holy Spirit is eternal, all-powerful, and all-knowing, and as mentioned earlier, He is the third person of the Trinity. The Holy Trinity represents the Christian understanding of God as three distinct persons in one divine essence, each revealing God's will and purpose. The Holy Spirit teaches and guides believers into all truth (Davis, 2024).

The Holy Spirit sanctifies the confessed believer. His role as the true Christ-follower is that of counselor and helper. He aids Christians in their weakness, desiring to intercede on their behalf, especially in moments when His presence, though ever-present, needs to be revealed. The Holy Spirit is the active presence of God in the lives of believers, with His characteristics and actions becoming evident in the individual (Sproul, 2014).

As a comforter, advocate, and helper, the Holy Spirit is often recognized as a source of assistance to believers. When times of trouble or need arise, the Holy Spirit comes alongside them to provide guidance, strength, and support (Davis, 2024). One of His greatest attributes is His ability to speak. This is vital, as His speech is often mistaken for a religious concept, but it should instead be viewed within the context of the relational dynamic between God and His people. God desires a relationship with His followers, and His responses to our questions, concerns, and prayers come through the Holy Spirit. Believers hear the Holy Spirit's guidance through various means: Scripture, prayer, visions or dreams, fellow Christians, and the still, small voice that resonates within the heart of each believer (Strange, 2023).

The Holy Spirit is also recognized as the teacher and guide for Christ's followers. He teaches and guides believers in understanding and living out the teachings of Jesus Christ, helping them interpret and apply the Scriptures to their lives. Within every believer, the Holy Spirit impacts the heart, especially when it comes to sin. Conviction, as a work of the Holy Spirit, reveals an individual's sinfulness, ultimately leading them to repentance and a turning toward God (Cross, 2007).

It is crucial to recognize that the Holy Spirit empowers believers to live out their Christian reality and fulfill their duties. This happens as the Spirit equips Christ's followers with spiritual gifts for service, enabling them to honor God's calling in their lives and live according to His will (Noyes, 2024).

To summarize, the Holy Spirit renews individuals, especially leaders, so they can have a positive influence on others. This influence is not simply about performing random acts of kindness, as we saw with those whom Jesus positioned to lead. Rather, it is about assisting others in recognizing the reality of who God is and how He works through our lives (Cross, 2007). This transformation is most profoundly seen when the Holy Spirit empowers believers to reflect the image of Christ. This, for many of us, is the greatest calling of a believer: to acknowledge, absorb, and publicly live out Christ-like characteristics. It's about living as Christ did and allowing our lives to impact others.

This is beautifully illustrated by Paul in 1 Corinthians 11:1, where he exhorts, "Imitate me, just as I also imitate Christ" (NIV). This statement addresses two key concerns: first, who and what we are as believers, and second, whether our lives are worthy of imitation by others (Hull, 2006). This transformation happens only when the Holy Spirit guides us, allowing us as leaders to demonstrate the very attributes Paul exemplified, reflecting their effectiveness. As leaders, we are called to be led by the Holy Spirit, demonstrating His power through our actions.

WHY THE HOLY SPIRIT IS IMPORTANT IN CHRISTIAN LEADERSHIP

With an improved understanding of the Holy Spirit, we now need to connect Him to Christian leadership. The Holy Spirit can be seen as the operating system for Christian leaders, meaning the way a leader functions is defined and driven by the Holy Spirit. Leaders who are successful in their roles do so because of the specific power that originates solely from the Holy Spirit. The Spirit equips leaders with the necessary gifts to fulfill their roles and responsibilities. Essential qualities—such as attributes, principles, and tools—are provided to enable leaders to make decisions in alignment with God's will, navigate challenging situations with compassion and integrity, and exemplify the fruit of the Spirit (Gal. 5:2223, NIV). These qualities, in turn, motivate and empower those who follow and receive guidance (Reiland, 2023).

For example, in the Old Testament, the Spirit of God came upon leaders who were called to oversee the construction of the Temple (Exodus 31:137:9, NIV). God's Spirit not only calls us into ministry but also equips us for the work. Many factors were involved in this calling: following instructions, envisioning and creating something that did not yet exist, developing and pouring into others, correcting and guiding those performing the task, and continually seeking assurance that God was satisfied with the project. Leaders, both then and now, face the same responsibilities—properly handling practices and procedures to ensure success in whatever God has ordained (Kuza, 2024).

Overall, the Holy Spirit is essential for leadership formation, stability, and success because He provides leaders with the necessary attributes, principles, and tools that define outstanding leadership (Mathew, 2017). Not only does He grant these qualities, but He also sustains them, refines them, and helps leaders utilize them at the appropriate times. This highlights the crucial need to depend on the Holy Spirit. Especially for leaders facing daily challenges, crises, and obstacles that hinder progress, the Holy Spirit strengthens them to turn to God and seek His intervention (Reiland, 2023). The Holy Spirit softens a leader's heart, enabling them to set aside pride and self-made solutions, and instead be receptive to God's guidance on what to do next (Barton, 1997). Through the Holy Spirit, God equips leaders with what is needed and empowers them to apply these gifts accurately, ensuring that the solutions to challenges prevent the failures that often arise (Watson B., 2024).

Uncle Frank's keychain reminds me of the role of the Holy Spirit, as He empowers leaders to extend themselves in various ways, using God-given gifts to open doors of opportunity for their followers. These opportunities lead to success, helping others recognize and understand God's hand in their personal and organizational endeavors. The Holy Spirit positions leaders to identify and stir up the gifts within them (2 Tim. 1:6, NIV), deploy disciple-makers, and empower those who proclaim the gospel (Kok, 2015). The seven gifts that this writing explores are the "keys" that the Holy Spirit distributes: prayer, faith, vision, integrity, knowledge, stewardship, and agape love.

When we think of the biblical leaders we admire, we see that those who experienced success possessed these gifts. Not only did they have them, but the Scriptures also show how they fulfilled their tasks through their proper use (Reiland, 2023). When these gifts were used correctly, they were organized, recognized, and applied appropriately with the help of the "key chain" – the Holy Spirit.

Take, for example, Joshua, who demonstrated great faith and wisdom as he succeeded Moses and led the Israelites into the promised land (Deut. 31:1-8, NIV). Or Elijah, who exhibited boldness, focus, and integrity during his confrontation with King Ahab to prove who the true God of Israel was (1 Kings 18:17-19, NIV). Similarly, consider the Apostle Paul when he stood before King Agrippa (Acts 26:1-29, NIV). Although he could have pleaded for his freedom, Paul instead recounted the history of society's rejection of Christ and used the opportunity to share the gospel with Agrippa and others present. His faith was evident as he boldly proclaimed the truth, trusting that God was still in control, regardless of the outcome (Sundar & Samuel, 2022).

These leaders accessed the gifts given to them, and through their leadership, they inspired followers and raised new leaders. Most importantly, their actions—guided by the Holy Spirit—brought glory to God, making their leadership worthy of emulation.

THE HOLY SPIRIT WELCOMED AND APPLIED

God equips leaders with these keys—though there are more than just the seven we've focused on—so that they can serve His church, Christian-based organizations, and His Kingdom worldwide. Paul reminds us that all our gifts are God-given (1 Corinthians 12:7-11, NIV) and are meant to be used for the good of the church and to glorify God. The call to leadership is established through God's Spirit, and it is the Holy Spirit who equips leaders to serve the people of God, ensuring that they depend fully on His working for more effective service (Kuza, 2024).

As a leader, I've faced many challenges that, with perseverance, have ultimately defined me as a successful Christian leader. I must admit, however, that some challenges were so overwhelming that I found myself questioning whether I should continue facing them or simply step aside and move on. Before stepping into leadership in the church, though, I was already a Christian, I encountered an experience that many early-stage leaders will face.

As a teenager, I worked at a well-known department store for a couple of years, navigating life after graduation and making decisions about what I wanted from the life I'd been given. For me, working was never a problem. I often had multiple jobs because I believed that wisely using my time, especially to make money, would make me a better person.

Nevertheless, I had worked at this store for a couple of years, and while the job itself was easy, the environment wasn't always so pleasant. It was the scripture, *"Delight yourself in the Lord" (Psalm 37:4, NIV)*, that gave me the strength to endure some of the disparaging, disrespectful, and even, at times, racist comments that were directed at me. Some of the staff, although not in positions of authority, believed it was their mission to put me "in my place" because of my race. Despite this, I persisted, relying on my faith.

Then, everything changed one day when, out of nowhere, we got a new manager. This was a man who had been quietly observing the store and its staff for weeks before he made his presence known. On the day he officially introduced himself, he announced that he would be holding private meetings with certain staff members. One of those meetings was with me.

At first, I was confused and thought the worst—that I was about to be let go. After all, I had seen some of my peers leave his office in tears, handing in their badges and work vests, leaving the store broken and hostile. When my turn came, I braced myself for bad news. But what happened next was completely unexpected.

The new manager shared a plan he had devised to take the store to new heights. He told me that he saw potential in me and wanted me to become an assistant manager. Though I had never considered it or had any interest in the position, he explained that he would train me in the store's business operations and provide mentorship on business and professional practices. He promised that if I committed myself, I would not fail, and in time, the store could be mine.

Shocked and unsure, I took a day to pray and seek advice. After some reflection and counsel, I agreed. The idea of becoming a manager was exciting, but I quickly realized that what lay ahead wasn't something a title alone could prepare me for. What awaited me would shape my perspective on leadership in ways I couldn't have imagined at the time.

Remember those colleagues of mine—the older know-it-alls who seemed determined to make my work experience miserable? Well, the transition into my new role immediately made me their boss and direct supervisor. The new manager was well aware of this, and, later on, I understood why he had positioned me in this role. He wanted to teach me something important about leadership and to see how I would respond in an uncomfortable situation.

So, on my first day as assistant manager, I showed up no longer in jeans and sneakers but in a suit and shoes. I humbly approached the team I was now supposed to lead, and right away, I encountered resistance and rejection. Despite the title and my new attire, they still saw the young man of the opposite race, who, in their eyes, should have been subservient to them, not in charge.

The point here, and the lesson I was meant to learn, was how I would respond. Immediately, I recalled a Bible lesson my grandmother had shared with me years ago about Moses when I had my struggles as a captain of my baseball team. Moses was called by God to lead a massive group of people, of various ages and outlooks, to God's promised land. On the surface, the task seemed straightforward. After all, they all desired the same outcome and knew what had to be done to achieve it. But, as most know, the journey was far from easy. The obstacles weren't just the typical challenges like the harsh landscape, dietary needs, and the fatigue and despair that arise when striving toward a difficult goal. The real problems came from the resistance and conflicting opinions of the people Moses was called to lead.

As I faced the challenging task of leadership, made even more difficult by the resistance of those I was called to lead,

I found myself reflecting on how Moses was able to push through similar struggles. Moses, in his leadership role, consistently turned to God for guidance and strength. God continually reminded him of his calling and reassured him that He had provided everything Moses needed to fulfill the task at hand. As long as Moses didn't try to "go it alone" and remain connected to God, He would guide him, empowering the gifts within him to ensure success.

On my first day as assistant manager, I knew I had to do the same. The very first thing I did was pray. I took time to remember all that God had done in my life, recalling that with Him, nothing is impossible. I reminded myself that there is no limit to what God can do, and I trusted that He would do it again.

The psalmist captures this truth so well when he declares: *"I will remember the deeds of the Lord; yes, I will remember your wonders of old. I will ponder all your work and meditate on your mighty deeds"* (Psalm 77:11–12, NIV). This scripture echoed in my heart as I stepped into that meeting. My petition to God was simple but earnest: I asked for strength and patience—strength to face what needed to be confronted, and patience to navigate the process. I prayed for wisdom to facilitate the necessary conversations, to cast a vision that would inspire the team, and to cultivate a collaborative spirit so we could walk together toward the shared goal of success.

The turnaround didn't happen overnight—patience remained a crucial part of the process—but as I stayed committed to my role and, most importantly, to God, I found myself empowered in unexpected ways. Through persistent prayer and trust in God's presence, He began to unlock specific principles, attributes, and tools within me. These weren't just theoretical concepts; they became active strategies that helped rebuild trust, foster a healthier workplace culture, and reshape how we operated as a team.

What I discovered is that when a leader remains yielded to God, He responds by imparting a degree of wisdom that often lies dormant until the moment of need. And when that wisdom is activated by the Holy Spirit, transformation becomes not only possible—it becomes inevitable.

God made it undeniably clear how vital integrity was—not just as a personal commitment, but as a leadership standard. I was to embody it, yes, but I was also to expect it from everyone on the team. Integrity wasn't optional; it was foundational.

As I wrestled with the lack of clarity and motivation among the team, God brought to mind a familiar passage of Scripture. The Israelites' failure to enter the Promised Land wasn't due to giants in the land—it was due to a lack of vision. They couldn't see beyond their fear, and as a result, forfeited God's promise. But Joshua saw differently. He held the vision. That vision burned within him and later became the very fuel that ignited the next generation to step into the inheritance God had prepared (Numbers 14:6-10, NIV).

At that moment, I understood—that vision starts with the leader. If I couldn't see what was possible, if I wasn't excited about what we were building, how could I ever expect those I was called to lead to be? The burden and beauty of vision belong to leadership.

It's our job to cast it, carry it, and communicate it.

And at the center of it all—God's love. That divine, agape love became my secret weapon. It enabled me to extend grace, choose forgiveness, and protect the sacred bond of unity among our team. No matter what was said or done, love became the compass that guided my responses. It was the glue that held us together through early resistance and helped us grow into something extraordinary.

By aligning with God's Spirit, implementing these principles, and leading with humility and hope, everything began to shift. The team dynamic transformed. Resistance broke. We didn't just become a good team—we became the *best* team in the store. We surpassed every metric, exceeded expectations, and even became the model for other teams both within our store and beyond.

As the accolades and congratulations began to pour in, I made one thing unmistakably clear: though the success came through me, it was never because of me. Every achievement, every turnaround, every milestone we reached—was only possible because of God.

Even at that young age, His Spirit was active in me, empowering me not only to lead but to empower others. What unfolded was far beyond what I could have manufactured on my own. The gifts He had placed within me—many of which I hadn't yet recognized—were awakened and activated by His Spirit. And through that divine empowerment, those gifts were used effectively to meet the needs of the moment and fulfill the task at hand.

That is what embodies effective leadership. When we use the gifts given by God, we not only fulfill the task at hand but also inspire and encourage those following us to become the next leaders. My colleagues at the department store grew to respect me, and I, in turn, gained new respect for them. They became like family as we moved forward together, accomplishing more and discovering God in all we did. When the "keys" God provides are not taken for granted but are consistently acknowledged and allowed to become a part of the leader's identity—at the guidance of the Holy Spirit—these keys will shape the leader's role. They prevent leadership fallout, such as dismissal, burnout, and stagnation, and ultimately lead to a leadership practice and engagement that impacts those God has entrusted to you, as you follow the greatest leader, Christ.

Seven Questions to Advance a Leader's Understanding of the Holy Spirit

1. Who is the Holy Spirit to you?

2. How would you define Spiritual discernment?

3. As a Christian leader, can you describe a specific situation where seeking the Holy Spirit's direction is crucial?

4. What Spiritual gift have you successfully utilized as a Christian leader?

5. Have you ever witnessed a Christian leader besides yourself rely on the Holy Spirit in their leadership endeavors? If so, please describe it.

6. Can you compare and contrast leadership with and without the empowerment and influence offered by the Holy Spirit in your leadership journey? Please describe.

7. Are you able, as a Christian leader, to discern between your thoughts and beliefs and the Holy Spirit's directives?

An Introduction to the Seven Keys

Thus far, I've shared my experience with Uncle Frank and how I witnessed the significance of possessing and properly utilizing entrance door keys. Uncle Frank had access to many doors, and what lay within those rooms—once opened—provided valuable content. But what stood out to me was that one could not access these offerings without first possessing the key, and once the key was provided, it had to be used correctly for an effective outcome.

Later in life, when I was blessed with my first administrative leadership role at the department store, I encountered moments of strife and disorganization. I knew there had to be something I could rely on to stabilize my focus and remain a confident, reliable authority figure—someone with an outlook toward success, while still maintaining humility and a servant's heart among the team. Just as Uncle Frank relied on his key chain, I quickly learned that I needed to turn to and depend on the Holy Spirit.

The key chain provided Uncle Frank with what was necessary to satisfy his duties. Early on in my assignment role, I began to see how the Holy Spirit equipped me with what I needed to lead effectively: attributes, principles, and tools, enabling me to thrive in my role, avoid defeat, and—through complete reliance on Him—achieve victories over my challenges. It was through this dependence that my leadership became truly effective.

As an assistant department store manager, I didn't fully recognize all the keys the Holy Spirit had distributed to me. In my ignorance, I eventually came to understand that this was part of the process of becoming an effective leader. It took time to acknowledge and embrace everything God was doing in me, as well as to identify the attributes, principles, and tools He had provided. In recognizing these gifts, I was reminded of the leadership calling reflected in the Old Testament, particularly in the positioning of the chief Artisan Bezalel.

"See, I have chosen Bezalel son of Uri, the son of Hur, of the tribe of Judah, (3) and I have filled him with the Spirit of God, with wisdom, with understanding, with knowledge, and with all kinds of skills— (4) to make artistic designs for work in gold, silver, and bronze, (5) to cut and set stones, to work in wood, and to engage in all kinds of crafts." (Exodus 31:2-5, NIV)

God called Bezalel to satisfy a specific task. Bezalel was a craftsman, meaning he had talent, and God knew this because He was the source of it. The Lord positioned him not only to utilize his design talents toward the formation of the Tabernacle, but God also ordained Bezalel to lead. He would, under the direction and power given by the Holy Spirit, lead others God sent to learn the skills he had, incorporate their talents with the task at hand, and they, under Bezalel's leadership, would successfully follow God's design and build all that God commanded (Boxx, 2020).

I would remain in department store management for five years, continuing to learn more about business while discovering and applying the unique gifts God had entrusted to me. After my first management role, I was promoted to store manager— something I had felt was foretold—and then to regional manager.

When I eventually left that organization, I ventured into entrepreneurship. Over the twelve years that followed, I saw more clearly how, whenever I turned to the Holy Spirit, He equipped me with keys, attributes, principles, and tools to enhance my leadership. God empowered me to be more effective in fulfilling the many tasks and responsibilities that come with leadership.

It was near the end of my business career when I realized that the keys I had been given were not taken away by the Holy Spirit. Instead, they remained with me, and as I still possessed them, He reminded me of what would be necessary moving forward and guided me on how to use them. As I pursued other ventures, I began to notice which keys I relied on most often and how, when used together, they produced results that far exceeded my expectations. Once again, it was my consistent desire to be guided by the Holy Spirit—and to work in unity with Him—that helped me more clearly identify these keys. They have come to define the strength and effectiveness of my leadership.

This writing now continues with the re-presentation of these keys, which will include a clear definition of each, a biblical reference, my personal testimony on their value, and the way they can and should be implemented. The keys I will share are limited to seven: prayer, faith, vision, integrity, wisdom, stewardship, and agape love. There are seven keys because the goal is for a leader to be whole, and seven represents Biblical completeness (Limburg, 1997). It is through the adoption of these seven keys, with the guidance and strengthening of the Holy Spirit, that you, as current and future Christian leaders of the world, will experience success and be recognized for your effective leadership.

Chapter Two
(Key One) Prayer

When I was a younger man, as mentioned earlier, I saw prayer or its practice regularly. To be clear, I saw prayer in action. What I did not see—or what was not explained to me—was the true purpose of prayer. In our services, the pastor or deacon would often lead the congregation in prayer. We would bow our heads and customarily say "Amen" when they concluded. We also frequently recited the Lord's Prayer, which I knew was from the Bible, but once again, what was emulated was the practice of prayer. However, I was far from understanding its true purpose.

I often recall, right before my ninth birthday, the day when our street was filled with people. Everyone was outside because the weather was perfect, and it seemed that whenever we were blessed with that ideal temperature—undisturbed by rain—it was as if the whole neighborhood was called to come outside and enjoy life. That's exactly what everyone was doing that day. We were in the streets, music blasting, someone had pulled out their BBQ grill, and another had gone to the local beer distributor, bought a bunch of quarter drinks, and put them on ice. The girls were playing double- dutch, some were dancing, and the boys were dribbling basketballs, waiting for their turn to challenge the winners of the previous game.

All in all, it was a perfect day—a day worth living and remembering, even as a young person who, according to the adults, "didn't know anything." It was perfect... until the unthinkable happened.

As we all enjoyed ourselves on the street, a car came barreling down the block at high speed. Most of us assumed it would eventually slow down like the others, but this car didn't. In fact, it seemed to speed up. Hand waves, gestures, and shouts for the driver to stop were ignored, and the car crashed into the table set up on the sidewalk, knocking over the bikes and scooters left there as we scrambled to the curb. Everyone made it to the sidewalk except for one girl—my dear friend Stacy.

It seemed to happen in slow motion. Everyone screamed for Stacy to look out, but it was too late. The car struck her, propelling her about twenty feet into the air, then sending her forward about sixty yards. She hit the ground with a loud thud, and though I had never witnessed anything like this before, I knew deep down this wasn't going to end well. She lay motionless as we rushed to her side.

As the car sped away, Stacy's mom ran out of the house, screaming, already fearing the worst. We gathered around her, and all we could see was Stacy, bleeding and twisted in unnatural positions, not moving. Her mother broke through the circle, tears streaming down her face, calling Stacy's name. But Stacy didn't respond. I thought she was dead.

"Call 911!" someone shouted, directing the plea to a building across the street. It was a small church that looked more like a shack. Someone outside shouted the 911 request into the church, and two women came running out. They pushed through the circle of onlookers to help Stacy and her heartbroken mother.

While the women attempted to comfort both Stacy and her mother, it was clear Stacy was unresponsive. One of the women, noticing this, gently asked the mother if she could pray while they waited for the ambulance. With tears in her eyes, the mother nodded, and the woman began to pray. Her words were heartfelt and powerful, moving everyone who stood nearby. Tears flowed freely, and even those who didn't typically attend church found themselves quietly offering praise.

As the prayer came to an end, with the usual, "In Jesus' name, Amen," the unthinkable happened. Stacy's eyes fluttered open, and moments later, she tried to move. The other woman gently held her back, urging her not to move. Miraculously, Stacy began to speak—first asking for her mom, then cracking a joke, just as she always did. Soon after, the ambulance arrived, and the paramedics carefully placed her on a stretcher. They took her to the local hospital, where the next chapter of her journey would begin.

The day in the street didn't end as any of us expected. It changed us. Most of us were initially stunned by the hit-and-run, but what truly shocked us was seeing Stacy regain consciousness, defying all odds, and appearing as though she might actually survive. In the moments after the accident, when we all spoke together, many of us had assumed she was gone.

It took five months, three surgeries, and a lot of rehabilitation, but eventually, Stacy came home. She had to relearn how to walk—and she did. It was nothing short of miraculous. She returned to school, and by the next year, we were all out there again, enjoying the beautiful weather, including Stacy, as though the accident, which could've been a tragedy, had never happened.

While Stacy was recovering, I would walk up the street to visit her. We talked about the elephant in the room—the accident. She asked if I had seen the entire thing and if I thought she was going to die. I told her honestly, "Yup." She then shared something with me that gave me chills. After the car hit her, she remembered flying through the air but couldn't recall anything after hitting the ground.

The next thing she remembered was hearing a voice asking God to return life to her.

"Artie," she said, "the next thing I knew, I could see. I saw people by my feet, a lady talking, and another holding my mom."

She continued, "I don't know much about what happened, but I do know this. The doctors and nurses who helped me over the last few months kept saying it was a miracle. They told me the car hit me at forty miles per hour, and they've never seen anyone survive that kind of impact. So, I've been sitting here, trying to figure out if it was just luck—or something else—that allowed me to live." As she spoke, it became clear to me why she had survived. I knew those women's prayers had been answered.

This was my first personal experience witnessing how God answers prayer and the profound spiritual power that surrounds such a connection. My friend was alive, and it was God who spared her because she had a purpose in His eyes. This experience opened my mind and heart to the significance of prayer, teaching me how essential it is in the life of someone who professes Christianity. It changed my life and reshaped my outlook on how I engage with God.

Years later, I ventured into different leadership roles. Because of everything I had witnessed with Stacy, I knew that prayer was crucial. God has given me a firsthand understanding of how He answers prayer and how circumstances change when He responds. This truth stayed with me in the days and weeks that followed. Without prayer, I realized I couldn't accomplish anything, but with prayer, the impossible could become reality. God delivers the miraculous when we pray. Even now, I am confident in this truth, as Stacy is alive and well today, knowing God and understanding how, through the prayers of the saints, the Lord responded and gave her what we could never provide for ourselves: restoration and life.

The Holy Spirit always initiates leadership for Christians, but true unity with God—and the essential dialogue that empowers leaders to succeed and remain strong—comes when we, as leaders, engage with God through prayer. This is why the first and most crucial key that Christian leaders need to access, possess, and regularly utilize is prayer.

PRAYER LIFE DEFINED

As a young Christian, my understanding of prayer was limited. To me, prayer was just a gesture—something people did at a specific time during a church service. While this is not wrong, it is a shallow view that can be harmful to both Christ's followers and Christian leaders. Misunderstanding prayer in this way prevents leaders from fully utilizing its power, from grasping what prayer truly does, and from realizing what it can lead to. For a long time, I saw prayer as a formality and didn't recognize the results it could bring beyond fulfilling a ritual. As a result, I misjudged its true power, how we as believers and leaders can and should draw from this gift, and why it is so crucial.

As I meet and spend time with many leaders today, I find that they face the same challenge I once had. For most, the difficulty with prayer lies in understanding what prayer truly is. Many leaders struggle to offer a clear definition. With this challenge in mind, let's first take a moment to define prayer.

Prayer is a central act for the Christian believer, involving the seeking and responding to the presence, will, purposes, and aid of God. It is an orientation toward the transcendent realm, allowing individuals to express their own and others' struggles, regrets, needs, and desires. This expression can occur in both individual and group settings, through verbal and nonverbal means, in conscious and unconscious states, and through both ritualized and non-ritualized methods (Cole, 2020). Additionally, prayer is a devout petition to God, involving spiritual communion. It often includes elements of worship, such as supplication, thanksgiving, adoration, or confession (Dictionary.com, 2024).

Prayer is the mutual contact between God and man. It is not limited to man contacting God; prayer also involves God reaching out to man (Lee, 2014). The term *prayer* comes from the Latin word *precarious*, meaning "obtained by begging," and *precari*, meaning "to entreat" (Holl, 1998). In Hebrew, prayer is translated as the verb *palal*, which means "to intervene," "mediate," or "judge" (Williams, 2021). The Hebrew noun for prayer is *tepillah*, meaning "to make a request" (Strongs, 1798). In Greek, several terms are used to describe prayer: *proseuchomai*, meaning "to pray" or "ask"; *proseuche*, meaning "to pray" or "speak with God"; and *deesis*, which refers to a petition, asking, or supplication made to God, often used in the context of a need (MacDonald, 2016).

According to the Westminster Shorter Catechism 98, prayer is "an offering up of our desires unto God, for things agreeable to his will, in the name of Christ, with confession of our sins, and thankful acknowledgment of his mercies" (Ligonier, 2024). This leads to the purpose of prayer, which must first be understood as a spiritual discipline that invites both individual and corporate outreach to God. Prayer, in this exchange, creates an expectation and anticipation: the petitioner expects God to hear their petition, and the petitioner also becomes receptive to hearing or receiving a response from God.

Prayer is one of the most common expressions of faith and devotion in the Christian life. Through prayer, individuals—and in this case, leaders—express their desires to God. However, these desires must align with God's will, for the Lord grants our requests only when they conform to His purpose. It's important to note that prayers do not change God's agenda, but they can change the circumstances a leader faces or those they are advocating for, as God intervenes in response to our requests.

Leaders should take comfort in knowing that God always knows what is best for His people and that He is working for our good and His glory, whether His answer is yes or no. This is why prayer is essential, especially for Christian leaders. Understanding and accepting God's "yes" and "no" enables our communion with Him to be truly beneficial—not just for our own agendas, but for the clarification of the agendas and desires of others.

Consider Abraham's prayer to God about Sodom. Abraham pleaded with God concerning His intention to destroy the city because of its sin (Gen. 18:16-33, NIV). While God's plan did not change, He did make it clear to Abraham that His prayer for the preservation of his nephew would be answered.

As seen with Abraham and countless others, prayer blesses leaders, strengthens them, and brings peace into their lives, reminding them that, no matter what happens, God is in complete control (Grandchamp, 2024). Through prayer, Christian leaders are reassured that God is with them and desires for them to succeed in their kingdom mission. They are covered and protected, especially in times of adversity. Prayer also nourishes leaders spiritually, helping them discern biblically and stay aligned with God's guidance (Williams, 2021). More than we as leaders could ever imagine, prayer opens our hearts for the Holy Spirit to lead us and guide us as we lead others.

At its core, prayer is simply the way we communicate with God. He, in turn, often uses prayer to speak to us. This communication is vital because it is how the Holy Spirit interacts with our leadership and directs how we operate as leaders. If we think of the Holy Spirit as our advocate, prayer is like a phone call that connects us with God. Through prayer, leaders receive their "agenda check-in" for regular updates, and within these conversations, God makes it clear whether our approach to leading His people is on track (Clinton, 2012).

Through prayer, our commitment to leadership is strengthened and refined. Our faith in God as leaders is empowered, allowing us to make necessary improvements in our leadership (Malphurs, 2002). Prayer also provides the unity needed to face opposition and achieve victory. Equally important, it keeps our will aligned with God's, which helps avoid many of the failures often seen in Christian leadership (Williams, 2021). When leaders maintain a continuous and consistent prayer practice, they are reminded of something crucial: We, as leaders, are not God.

DANIEL

When Daniel is discussed in the Bible, the many qualities attributed to him often do not include the title of "leader." However, despite this common oversight, God did not miss it—and neither did one other individual: King Nebuchadnezzar of Babylon. As the reigning oppressor during the early years of Judah's exile, Nebuchadnezzar recognized Daniel's leadership abilities.

Daniel's journey in Babylon began when he, along with other exceptional young men from Judah, was selected to serve in various capacities for King Nebuchadnezzar. When a decree was issued by the king that led to the execution of numerous wise men, magicians, astrologers, sorcerers, and Chaldeans—who failed to interpret Nebuchadnezzar's troubling dream—Daniel stepped forward. He provided the king with a correct interpretation and understanding of the dream. In response, the king promoted Daniel to a leadership position in his kingdom.

The king said to Daniel, "Surely your God is the God of gods and the Lord of kings and a revealer of mysteries, for you were able to reveal this mystery" (Daniel 2:47, NIV). The king then elevated Daniel to a high rank, lavishing him with gifts. He made him ruler over the entire province of Babylon and placed him in charge of all its wise men (Daniel 2:48, NIV).

Despite the passage of time and the change in Babylon's leadership, Daniel's character and position continued to flourish. Under King Darius, Daniel became governor and impressed the king with his leadership. Darius recognized that "Daniel distinguished himself among the administrators and satraps by his exceptional qualities, and the king planned to set him over the entire kingdom" (Daniel 6:3, NIV). Unfortunately, this provoked jealousy among others who lacked the qualities that Daniel displayed in the king's eyes. They conspired to find a charge against him regarding his honorable work in the kingdom. However, because Daniel was upright, they could find nothing to accuse him of.

In the end, the conspirators realized what was truly meaningful to Daniel—what gave him strength, direction, and the qualities that made him the admired leader he was: his commitment to prayer. They concluded that if they could undermine Daniel's ability to pray, they could break him.

This group of individuals—what we might today call "haters"—went to King Darius. After excessively flattering him, they deceived him into establishing a decree that any prayer within the kingdom should be directed solely toward the king. In his ignorance, Darius agreed, and the decree was set in motion. Word soon reached Daniel, who, despite the new law, "went home to his upstairs room where the windows opened toward Jerusalem. Three times a day, he got down on his knees and prayed, giving thanks to his God, just as he had done before" (Daniel 6:10, NIV).

Even though the new decree clearly stated the consequences of noncompliance, Daniel continued to pray openly, as he always had. This act of defiance led to his arrest. Following the decree, Darius reluctantly cast Daniel into the lion's den, believing that the young leader would meet his end there, satisfying the conspirators' desires (Rigney, 2022).

Many might have thought that, given the new law and its deadly consequences, prayer wasn't worth the risk. Some might have prayed quietly, privately, in hopes of avoiding such drastic consequences. But Daniel chose a different path—one that every leader should follow. He valued and understood that his communication with God defined who he was. He wasn't confused about the matter; to him, prayer was essential because it aligned him with the purpose God had placed on his life (Wilkin, 2023). Daniel knew that without prayer, he would be nothing. He understood that every success he experienced as a leader was directly tied to his regular connection with God through prayer.

Daniel's leadership shares many similarities with those leading churches and industries today. Though his position was unconventional, Daniel possessed attributes that even his enemies recognized as valuable. Remember, Nebuchadnezzar initially sought young Jewish men who exemplified God-like character. After witnessing the unique gifts that Daniel and his three friends possessed, they were promoted to leadership roles in what could be considered uncharted waters. Imagine being a leader in enemy territory—responsible for shaping the daily lives of people, even those whose culture was oppressive to your own.

Despite these challenging circumstances, Daniel remained steadfast, consistently rising above and beyond his peers. As he interacted more with the rulers of Babylon, he continued to be promoted to higher positions. Yet, what remained most significant about Daniel's leadership—despite the unorthodox nature of his rise—was his unwavering relationship with God. This relationship thrived because of the regular communication he had with God. In simple terms, Daniel saw prayer not just as a ritual, but as a priority for his survival, success, influence, and impact as a leader. It wasn't just about leading those under his guidance; it was about setting an example for his brethren, whom God had positioned to follow in his footsteps.

Daniel's approach to prayer was also profound. While we can assume he prayed while in the lion's den, the Bible reveals that he prayed long before the penalty for breaking the prayer restriction came. Interestingly, Daniel anticipated that trouble might follow.

Instead of denying the power of prayer or shrinking from the consequences, he embraced the very resource that prayer offers. Daniel understood the value of prayer: it provides intimacy with God and allows for intercession before God (Bishop & McKaughan, 2023).

With intimacy, we draw close to the Lord, never abandoned, even when loneliness threatens our ability to lead. Prayer opens the door for intercession, allowing God to step in and deliver what we need—even when we don't know what we need (Platt, 2019). In times of confusion, and struggle, and when a leader's role or life is under threat, prayer is a divine resource that equips us with everything required to persevere.

Think about Daniel. Though we often see his outward confidence in facing the decree and how it directly contradicted his identity, his strength wasn't solely from himself. Prayer was sacred to Daniel because, through it, he was reminded of the deep unity he shared with God. It was through prayer that his connection with the Divine was not only affirmed but strengthened, especially during moments of profound challenge.

Through Daniel's example, we are reminded that prayer not only connects us with God but also provides the guidance and understanding needed to respond effectively when leadership demands attention across various situations. As leaders, we often have answers born from experience, but we don't have all the answers. As Christian leaders, we know who does, and prayer serves as our "direct connection" to God, who is our refuge and strength, an ever-present help in times of trouble (Psalm 46:1, NIV).

Prayer also acts as a preventative measure, averting problems before they arise, while also establishing peace in the midst of challenges. It activates the advocate God has provided, ensuring that we are never alone in our leadership roles. When we feel depleted, prayer allows us to encounter God, and through His deliverance, we are empowered to glorify Him (Psalm 50:15, NIV).

As Daniel demonstrated, incorporating prayer as a regular part of a leader's approach—especially when practiced proactively—ensures continuous communication with God and a steadfast acknowledgment that He is in control. As Christian leaders, we must understand that, as

Daniel experienced, prayer may come with a cost. However, as we saw from Daniel's response to the restriction, the cost is undoubtedly worth it. This is why an intimate prayer life is not merely a suggestion for leaders; it is a vital necessity, a gift graciously given by God. Leaders cannot lead on their own. God must walk with them, speak with them, and equip them with what they need to fulfill the calling of leadership.

Why Prayer is Important to Leadership

I genuinely don't believe any Christian leader would purposely discount prayer, claiming it isn't important. However, I do think that many leaders fail to prioritize prayer, as the daily challenges and routines they face often distract them from adequately connecting with God. We see an example of this from the greatest leader to ever live—Jesus Himself. When the time for His crucifixion drew near.

He left His disciples and went to the Garden of Gethsemane. There, "He fell with His face to the ground and prayed, 'My Father, if it is possible, may this cup be taken from me. Yet not as I will, but as You will'" (Matt. 26:39, NIV). Understanding the immense suffering ahead and the separation from the Father, Jesus sought empowerment through prayer to fully fulfill His will.

This is why prayer is vital for Christian leaders. Prayer empowers us to fully utilize the gifts God has given us so that His will can be accomplished through us. Prayer requires complete dependence on God, fostering humility, obedience, and a heightened awareness of His presence, especially as we lead (Martin, 2019). As demonstrated by Christ, a crucial aspect of our leadership responsibility is to pray. Prayer strengthens our ability to obey God's instructions, enabling us to carry out His calling with supernatural strength beyond our natural abilities, through the "keys" of the Holy Spirit.

A leader who maintains a strong prayer life has a profound impact on the lives of those they serve. Even Christian leaders cannot bear the weight of leadership for long without recharging their spirits through communion with God. A significant aspect of Jesus' mission was to foster spiritual growth in His disciples, helping them understand His oneness with the Father and preparing them for their calling. He relayed that the same relationship and dialogue with God, essential for accomplishing His will, is available to them through prayer (Taketa, 2011).

Prayer, once again, acknowledges a leader's dependence on God, who empowers them to use their God-given gifts more effectively to accomplish their tasks. Jesus Himself prayed when faced with important decisions, difficult situations, disappointments, and moments when He needed to intercede for His disciples. His ministry demonstrated the importance of constant communion with God, a communion that was always centered on prayer (Wengler, 2021).

Christian leaders must follow Jesus' example, as our role is to guide people from where they are to where God is calling them to be. Leaders are meant to help those they lead to develop a Godinspired perspective and move toward the purpose God has designed for them in His kingdom (Taketa, 2011). Through constant guidance from God, leaders can be confident in what they teach, how they minister, and how they lead. While a leader's knowledge, skills, and talents are valuable assets, they are incomplete without consistent communion with God, which is nourished through continual prayer.

PRAYER APPLICATION

I have been driven many times to my knees by the overwhelming conviction that I had nowhere else to go. My own wisdom and that of all about me seemed insufficient for that day." — **Abraham Lincoln** (*Noah Brooks, 2017*)

This testimony, shared by one of America's most revered leadership figures, highlights how vital prayer is to the success of a leader. When those called to lead engage in conversational prayer with God, their true motivations are revealed, and the Holy Spirit often provides specific insights that support a more balanced leadership approach (Demaria, 2020). For the Christian leader, a committed prayer life yields tremendous rewards. Prayer helps bring into focus the very benefits that contribute to effective leadership. As you petition God for His grace, mercy, and direction in every area of your life and work, His presence in your life will naturally extend to those you interact with (Warden, 2023).

Leaders who are devoted to prayer regularly experience the following:

1. Alignment with God

As demonstrated by Christ, prayer enables us to align with His will.

Leaders are called to set aside their own desires and submit fully to God's direction. Through prayer, we become exposed to what God speaks, reveals, and requires. It is through this intimate dialogue that we ask, seek, and discern His will. In response, God makes His ways and plans known.

2. Spiritual re-strengthening.

Whether we admit it or not, leaders are often left feeling dismal— broken and weary. Many give their all, while some followers take everything a leader has to offer. Consider Christ on the cross, who, even in His final moments, was asked to save the repentant thief. At His lowest, there was still an expectation—at least a minimum need—He was asked to meet. A similar burden is often placed on today's Christian leaders. In such moments, prayer becomes essential for the revitalization leaders so deeply need, especially in times of challenge. Prayer reminds leaders of God's power and peace, both of which help them endure and overcome. While prayer may not instantly remove a leader's struggle, it helps reveal how God is reinforcing the use of specific tools He has already provided. Many of the additional gifts He offers— patience, joy, peace, and perseverance—serve to guide leaders toward lasting success and help prevent the breakdown or failure in Christian leadership referenced earlier.

3. A desire to project humility.

Prayer conditions a leader to remain humble. Many leaders experience long-term failure because they forget who they are in light of who Jesus is. A lack of humility is often the very ingredient that leads to leadership disruption and downfall. This often stems from overconfidence—when leaders grow too accustomed to success and achievement, they may become complacent, no longer seeking God's guidance, approval, or correction. In these moments, leaders may foolishly rely on their own strength, neglecting to engage in meaningful communion with God.

However, when prayer remains a priority—regardless of our condition—leaders acknowledge their need for God. There is a continual confession that His leadership defines theirs. Prayer not only uncovers weaknesses but also calls leaders to greater trust and dependence on God.

Remember what the apostle Paul said regarding weakness and humility:

"That is why, for Christ's sake, I delight in weaknesses, in insults, in hardships, in persecutions, in difficulties. For when I am weak, then I am strong." *(2 Cor. 12:10, NIV)*

4. Spiritual protection and openness to Biblical tutelage.

Though mentioned earlier, it bears repeating: prayer not only positions leaders to seek God but also provides spiritual protection and tutelage when most needed. This divine guidance helps leaders stay aligned with the path the Lord has set for them. Leaders are often tempted by alternatives that, at first glance, may not appear to conflict with God's purposes. However, when we stray on our own, the consequences often become clear only after destruction and dismay have taken their toll. Prayer binds leaders to God, reminding them that they belong to Him. It is God who aims to protect and govern, helping leaders avoid temptation in all its forms. Leaders are vulnerable to pride, selfishness, impatience, lust, and greed. In prayer, they must openly reveal their vulnerability, acknowledging that they cannot lead effectively apart from God. In doing so, the protection and instruction He offers can guard their hearts and minds. This makes prayer a vital "key" to sustaining godly leadership (Wilson, 1994).

5. Access to and the means to effectively use the spiritually gifted keys.

Speaking of keys, prayer provides access to the very subject of this writing—the keys to effective leadership. It begins with communication, for the heart of leadership is the communication between God and the Christian leader. Prayer allows leaders to understand God's purposes and plans for what He calls them to do. But prayer also gives us the space to listen, where God reminds us, *"You already have what you need to do this."* Often, what we need are the keys discussed in this writing (Clinton, 2012). Prayer convinces us that if we turn to our "keychain," God will direct us to the tools we need, guide us in how to use them and empower us to wield them effectively.

This process also brings forth something else from God: discernment. Discernment is the ability to make sound, moral judgments, recognize the moral implications of different situations, and evaluate potential courses of action. It includes the ability to assess the moral and spiritual state of individuals, groups, and even movements (Ferguson, 2023). Discernment aids in determining where and how the "keys" are to be used, ensuring that a leader's approach to their duties will be seen as effective and in alignment with God's will.

Seven Questions to Advance the Understanding of Prayer for Christian Leadership Success

1. In what ways has prayer impacted your leadership?
2. As a leader, in what way do you believe prayers can guide your decision-making?
3. Are there specific areas of your leadership approach that need more prayer consideration than others?
4. In what way can prayer help you as a leader navigate through difficult situations?
5. How would you go about balancing your personal prayer needs with the prayer petitions and responsibilities of the church or organization you lead?
6. What do you believe are the limitations of a leader when prayer is not regularly utilized?
7. Based on your recommendation, what prayer practice would support a healthy leadership role?

Chapter Three
(Key Two) Faith

Every Christian leader has at least one defining moment early in their ministry—a story that changed the course of their ministry and, through that experience, transformed the way they see God. My story took place during the development stage of my ministry while I continued my entrepreneurial work. At the time, I owned several cellular phone stores, and though I knew God was leading me further into ministry, it was my responsibilities (or, to be honest, my resistance) that delayed the full transition from one profession to God's calling.

God had made His intentions clear about four years earlier, revealing that my first ministry assignment was to host and lead a weekly Bible study. Right from the start, I resisted, offering multiple excuses, all of which were unmerited. At first, I could sense God's response to my defiance was similar to when my mom would direct me to do something, and I would refuse to comply—God said nothing. In fact, I came to understand that God often grows silent until we obey. Once I realized that my avoidance of what God wanted me to do was causing me to experience the discontentment that comes with conviction, I repented and went the way God wanted me to go.

Once humbled, I asked the question that many reluctant leaders ask: *"How exactly am I to do what You demand, Lord?"*

The Lord wanted me to establish a Bible study meeting, and I came to understand that it was to be held weekly at the downtown store I owned. To some degree, I understood what God was asking of me, and by then, I had reached a point in life where pleasing Him had become my priority. But when it came to this Bible study, I wrestled with doubts. First, who was I to conduct a Bible study? Though I was somewhat familiar with scripture, could I teach effectively with just knowing the basics? Because of this, I questioned my qualifications for the task. I also thought, what would make people take this offering seriously, especially given my background as a former secular entertainment professional and a local business owner?

My greatest objection, however, was the question of why anyone would come to be a part of it. In my area of Long Island, church, Jesus, and the Bible weren't as central in the lives of my neighbors as they had been in my youth. Additionally, I wondered how I would even get the word out about this Bible study. Though I knew it would be disobedient, part of me wanted to disregard the idea entirely, convinced that it would fail.

Then, out of nowhere, God's response came—one that included correction, clarity, and direction. It fell upon me like a ton of bricks.

God answered me with the precision that only He could deliver: *"Establish the date, create an invitation with your direct phone number on it, and go buy four cases of bottled water."* My initial response was, *"Huh?"* But, as always, I aimed to please God. I did exactly as He instructed, and then I received the next directive: *"Stand at the street corner below the traffic signal. When the light turns red, walk down the street with bottled water and offer it to drivers."*

So, the directive was to hand out bottled water to each driver and anyone in their vehicle who asked. While sharing water, I was also to give them an invitation to the Bible study. Though I didn't fully understand where this would lead, I obeyed, trusting that it would please God. The first day, in 92-degree heat, I went outside and did exactly as I was told. I handed out ice-cold bottled water for free to drivers stuck at the delayed traffic light, each bottle wrapped with an invitation to the Bible study set to take place four weeks later. On the first day, I handed out about forty bottles. The second day, I gave out another forty. The following week, I distributed fifty bottles, and then, something unexpected happened: my phone rang with someone interested in attending. Encouraged, I returned to the street, handed out another fifty bottles, and the phone continued to ring. Though the number of people was small, it was far more than I had expected. By the last week, I had confirmation from twelve attendees, nine of whom actually showed up on the first night. We had one of the most incredible meetings centered on biblical topics I'd ever had.

When it was all said and done, all I could say was how amazing God is. I was, and still am, in awe of how He made something that seemed impossible happen.

This experience led me to recall Naaman's encounter with Elisha while seeking a cure for his leprosy. Naaman's wife's servant had heard of a healer in Samaria, and so Naaman traveled from Aram to seek him out. When he arrived at the house of the prophet Elisha, he had a preconceived notion of how the healing process would unfold. However, Elisha, who did not meet Naaman face to face, sent a servant with detailed instructions for his healing. The command was simple: *"Go, wash yourself seven times in the Jordan, and your flesh will be restored, and you will be cleansed"* (2 Kings 5:10, NIV).

Naaman, however, was taken aback by Elisha's lack of personal engagement and the simplicity of the instructions. His disappointment seemingly grew as he dismissed the directions, thinking that following them would not lead to his healing. Naaman began to rationalize other alternatives, suggesting he could bathe in.

"Better rivers," or that Elisha should come out and perform spiritual gestures to resolve his issue. After some persuasion from his servants, Naaman reluctantly obeyed, and when he dipped into the Jordan for the seventh time, his leprosy was healed—just as Elisha had said.

"Set a date, create an invitation, and buy four cases of water. Then, stand in the street and hand them out." I felt like Naaman, thinking, *"This doesn't make much sense."* I also, like him, thought, *"God, can't You just do such and such or bring me an event planner?"* But God never answered my inquiries. Instead, He remained silent until I did what I was told to do. Once it was done, and I saw the result, it all began to make sense.

This wasn't about the water, or the flyers, or even the Jordan River.

For me, it was about simply going out and doing what God said. For Naaman, it was about obeying God's command. When we do what God tells us, even when it doesn't make sense and doesn't add up according to our own reasoning, we come to understand that success is not by our will or power. It is all due to God. However, God asks for something from us to make these miracles our reality: obedience.

And our obedience to God in moments such as these is a demonstration of what is called faith.

By standing in ninety-degree heat, handing out bottles of water, and by Naaman jumping into the unfiltered Jordan River, both of us were demonstrating our faith. By acting without seeing the immediate outcome, we were choosing to believe and trust that what God asked of us would lead to the result He promised. What God demands from us is to see the unseen and to trust Him to bring about what we cannot achieve on our own. This act of trusting without visible evidence is called faith.

Faith was my lesson that day, and I will never forget its value. I'm sure Naaman didn't forget it, either. It takes faith to lead because many times, leadership requires us to move forward into places and toward outcomes that are not visible. When those outcomes are not visible, and we trust God to direct our steps, what is necessary to continue is what God seeks from us: faith.

FAITH DEFINED

The first time I heard the word *faith* wasn't during the experience I've shared earlier, nor was it in church. Surprisingly, I wasn't introduced to the term *faith* in a spiritual context at all. The first time I recall hearing the word was as a child, while living with my mom. Like me, my mom had an affinity for music, and I remember being about ten years old, walking into the house to find her cleaning the kitchen while dancing along to a song titled "Faith" by the famous singer George Michael.

The hook of the song talked about the necessity of having faith. Of course, the faith he was referring to was far different from the biblical faith we're discussing here. But this early encounter with the term shows how easily the word can be misunderstood or misapplied. Later, when faith was explained to me in a more biblical context, I realized that Michael's 1987 hit could have easily been mistaken for a church song! It became clear to me that there was a lot more to faith than what George Michael's song had conveyed.

So, what exactly is faith? While there are multiple definitions, they all connect to a similar foundation. Author and theologian C.S. Lewis approaches faith from two perspectives: as a belief and as a virtue. As a belief, he suggests that faith reflects one's acceptance of the doctrines of Christianity as true. As a virtue, faith is the ability to hold onto things your reason once accepted, despite changing moods or circumstances (Lewis, 1980).

Vines offers a similar perspective. In the Hebrew language, faith is reflected by the term *emunah*, which means certainty and faithfulness. In Greek, the term *pistis* is used, which signifies a form of persuasion or conviction based on hearing (Strongs, 1798). It also involves having belief and trust in what is spoken and illustrated.

While this writer agrees with the definitions mentioned earlier, we lean more heavily on the biblical explanation of faith. The writer in Hebrews states that faith is *"confidence in what we hope for and assurance about what we do not see"* (Hebrews 11:1, NIV). This passage is rooted in the *faithfulness* of the Old Testament saints, many of whom held onto God's promises concerning the future of Israel—the promise of a special land and a salvific Messiah. Though they didn't know if they would see the fulfillment of these promises in their lifetime, they responded to God in faith, allowing their belief in Him to shape their continued devotion (Malphurs, 2003).

In essence, faith is about continuing to trust in God, even when feelings and circumstances suggest otherwise. The alternative— disbelief—often feels appealing, but such impressions aim to drive us away from God. In contrast, faith involves confidence in who God is, in what He has said, and in His promises. Faith is simply to believe God (Magnelli, 2020).

Through faith, the believer—and in our case, the leader—draws on both the evidence of God's faithfulness in the past and the proof they experience in their own life. This trust allows the leader to remain steadfast, rooted in God's identity. This is why faith is often closely related to trust. The concepts of faith and faithfulness parallel trust and trustworthiness, and they are often used interchangeably (Bishop & McKaughan, 2023).

A leader's outlook may not always be clear, but with complete dependency on God, they can move forward to achieve their God-given agenda. However, as they advance, they will inevitably face disruption, delays, and unforeseen challenges. Leaders empowered by the Holy Spirit, with faith as one of His key offerings, will continue to press forward toward the goals that God has set. The beneficiaries of this perseverance will not only be the leader but also those God has positioned to follow them.

An example of this can be seen in the leadership struggles of Jehoshaphat. After a troubling encounter with Israel's late leader, Ahab, Jehoshaphat was faced with a serious threat from the combined forces of the Ammonites and Moabites. With their vast numbers, Judah seemed defenseless and unlikely to prevail. However, Jehoshaphat turned to God in prayer, and God responded through the prophet Jahaziel, saying:

"Do not be afraid or discouraged because of this vast army. For the battle is not yours, but God's. Tomorrow, march down against them. They will be climbing up by the Pass of Ziz, and you will find them at the end of the gorge in the Desert of Jeruel. You will not have to fight this battle. Take up your positions; stand firm and see the deliverance the Lord will give you, Judah and Jerusalem. Do not be afraid; do not be discouraged. Go out to face them tomorrow, and the Lord will be with you." (2 Chronicles 20:15-17, NIV)

God instructed Jehoshaphat to go to the battle lines and remain steadfast. They were not to waver because the battle was not theirs, but the Lord's. Now, Jehoshaphat had the task of convincing the people of Judah to step forward, seemingly as targets, and then to stand firm, trusting that God would handle the battle. What became evident here was that the only way they would know if God's promise was true was by following His command. To march into battle with no intention to fight and no weapon to wield would require complete faith and trust in God's word.

Jehoshaphat and Judah did just that. When they went out, he placed the worshippers at the front, leading them in praises to God. And God's word came to pass. He set ambushes against all those who opposed Judah, causing their enemies to turn on each other. Without Judah having to lift a finger, their enemies were defeated. Once the dust settled, Judah reaped the rewards of their faith. With all their enemies destroyed, the spoils of victory were theirs.

Faith is a key ingredient in the emergence of a leader (Clinton, 2012). This is evident in the way faith empowered Jehoshaphat to lead his nation from defeat. Likewise, faith is essential for leading Christ's followers toward the blessings God has in store. This same faith is what Christian leaders need to remain steadfast during difficult times, preventing failure. Moreover, faith allows them to overcome challenges and press forward, achieving the many things that God has predetermined as part of their success—whether for their church, organization, industry, or the Kingdom of God.

Christian leaders must have the ability to see the invisible, believe in the incredible, and accomplish the impossible (Thomson, 2017). Leaders need faith. Faith is about completely relying on who Jesus is and allowing Him to direct our steps in the missions He has established.

Not only do leaders need to possess faith, but they must also demonstrate it. As Luther says, "Faith is a living, bold trust in God's grace, so certain of God's favor that it would risk death a thousand times trusting in it. Because of it, you freely, willingly, and joyfully do good to everyone, serve everyone, suffer all kinds of things, and love and praise the God who has shown you such grace" (Luther, 2010). What Luther describes is the essence of leadership, encompassing both the fortunate and undeserved outcomes that leaders often face. However, the willingness to endure and achieve what a Christian leader is called to accomplish comes through a total reliance on God.

This reliance becomes a reality only when faith is a central element of a Christian leader's design. Faith, therefore, is not just an internal belief but an act of the heart and the strength that should guide our lives, lived according to the Scriptures and with openness to both the present and, most importantly, to God (Tamas, 2017). It is through this kind of faith that Christian leadership is empowered, making it effective.

ABRAHAM

The Bible offers many examples of individuals whose lives were defined by faith, and one of the most recognizable figures in this regard is Abraham. When faith is discussed in connection with Abraham, the most obvious example that comes to mind is his willingness to take his only son, Isaac, up Mount Moriah in obedience to God and prepare to sacrifice him. Just as Abraham was about to carry out the act, an angel intervened, instructing him not to proceed but instead to sacrifice a nearby ram (Gen. 22:2-14, NIV).

However, rather than focusing on this well-known story, this writer is drawn to examine an earlier experience in Abraham's life— before he was even identified as Abraham.

Abram, his wife, and his entire family, led by his father, journeyed from Ur of the Chaldeans toward the land of Canaan.

They settled in Haran, but there, Abram's father passed away. It was in Haran that the Lord spoke to Abram, saying:

"Go from your country, your people, and your father's household to the land I will show you. (2) I will make you into a great nation, and I will bless you; I will make your name great, and you will be a blessing. (3) I will bless those who bless you, and whoever curses you I will curse, and all peoples on earth will be blessed through you." (Gen. 12:1-3)

It was Abram's response to God that truly demonstrated what we recognize as faith. First, there is no biblical record suggesting that Abram had prior knowledge of God. However, when Abram heard God's voice, he felt the need to obey, and he departed as the Lord instructed. Abram's leadership began with this act of obedience, as his departure included his wife Sarai, his nephew Lot, and the people they had gathered in Haran. At the age of seventy-five, Abram left Haran with all that he owned and led his family to the unknown land of Canaan (Gen. 12:4-9, NIV). Because of his obedience, God promised him that his descendants would possess this land. It was through this promise and Abram's unwavering faith that the people of God would be formed, and the sacred land, which would become Israel and Jerusalem, would be the foundation of the Christian faith.

From the beginning, God's call and Abram's obedient decision to embrace that call—venturing into the land of Canaan—demonstrated and initiated many powerful moments of faith to come (York, 2003). Key facts about this often-underappreciated moment include the reality that Abram departed willingly. He left not only his land but also a large portion of his family. He walked away from everything familiar, everything that offered him comfort, to go to a place he had never seen, among people he had never met, all in honor of a promise from God—a God with whom it's assumed he had little to no prior relationship. The key thing about Abram is that he trusted God (Heaster, 2021). Why? We don't know for certain, but what is clear is that he did. He left everything behind to pursue something he couldn't see. Faith does this to humans and, more specifically, to leaders. It's also important to note that Abram didn't make this journey alone. He had company—his wife, nephew, and servants—whom he was responsible for. Once again, Abram was leading people to an unknown land, yet he believed the journey and the risk was worth it because of his faith in God.

WHY FAITH IS IMPORTANT TO CHRISTIAN LEADERSHIP

As those at the forefront of Godly missions, Christian leaders are called to exemplify care, humility, and courage. This becomes possible only when they are led by the faith that God has provided.

Through this faith, they are enabled to serve, offer comfort during times of instability, and inspire when retreat seems like the most reasonable option. Faith supports leaders by strengthening both their confidence and humility—two essential components of Christian leadership (Blair, 2023). It also empowers them to make ethically sound decisions, to encourage followers through difficult times, and to cultivate an environment where every individual is valued and respected (Mujuru, 2023). One such ethical decision arises when the organization, community, or family they lead must move forward- a movement when followers need to feel encouraged, respected, and deeply valued.

Development, as previously mentioned, is a key objective for leaders—especially within the Christian context. Whether it involves personal growth, organizational progress, improvements in practices and procedures, or—within the church—congregational development, all such efforts by Christian leaders must align with God's voice. Once the Word is received, the confidence God provides should become the driving force behind the leader's forward movement. That same confidence must then be passed on—and even multiplied—among those who have committed themselves to the shared journey. All of this is made possible when leaders access, and intentionally place at the forefront, the faith that God has granted to all who lead.

The faith being described here involves advancement—moving forward and acting on our beliefs with radical trust and complete dependence on God. Leaders trust that God will guide them to where they need to be and shape them into who they are called to become, because the Lord Himself is faithful (Hallock, 2023). Abraham exemplified this. God called him out of Haran to a land he had never seen, never visited, and knew nothing about. Yet Abraham not only followed God's instruction, but he also led others into that unknown place, showing confidence as the one positioned at the front. He possessed what was necessary to fulfill his calling because he placed his full trust in God (Redmond, 2017). It is this act of trusting the Lord and stepping forward with conviction that transforms someone positioned in front into a leader called by God. When we walk by faith in ministry, we rely on God's steadfast love and faithfulness—not only in our own lives, but in the life of the church as well (Hallock, 2023).

Just as Abraham did not know what awaited him in Canaan, Christian leaders today—walking in faith—may not know what lies ahead on the other side of God's command or beyond the tasks He directs them to fulfill. Faith not only empowers the leader to move forward; it also equips them with the necessary qualities to journey alongside those involved. Whether they are congregants, investors, or family—like Abraham's—leaders who move according to God's call, share their faith with the sacred individuals God has placed around them. And through the leader's example of faith, those individuals begin to believe and trust in God in ways that mirror the leader's own trust.

Leaders can draw motivation from Joshua, who stepped into Israel's leadership after Moses' death. As he led a new generation into battle to claim the land, he faced the fortified city of Jericho. In that moment, the Lord provided an unconventional strategy: march around the city to bring about its collapse. Scripture details God's instructions:

"See, I have delivered Jericho into your hands, along with its king and its fighting men. March around the city once with all the armed men. Do this for six days. Have seven priests carry trumpets of rams' horns in front of the ark. On the seventh day, march around the city seven times, with the priests blowing the trumpets. When you hear them sound a long blast on the trumpets, have the whole army give a loud shout; then the wall of the city will collapse, and the army will go up, everyone straight in." (Joshua 6:2–5, NIV)

If Joshua had any doubts, Scripture does not record them. Taking the Lord at His word, he carried out the commands exactly— and the walls came tumbling down. What must be remembered is that Joshua did not alter, question, or revert the instructions he received. Though they may have seemed unorthodox, he believed what God said, trusted in what the Lord instructed, and placed his full faith in Him—confident that what God promised would come to pass. All Christian leaders must respond in the same way to witness the fulfillment of what is anticipated. As James reminds us, *"You must believe and not doubt, because the one who doubts is like a wave of the sea, blown and tossed by the wind"* (James 1:6, NIV).

Faith not only empowers Christian leaders to believe, but it also empowers them to respond. It's one thing to express one's faith verbally, but it's entirely different—and far more impactful—when a leader responds to their faith through action. We saw this with Abraham when he left Haran in obedience to God's call. We saw it again with Joshua when he followed God's directives concerning Jericho. The outcomes reveal the power of such faith. Abraham advanced, and his advancement led to him being called a friend of God. It was his faith that inspired others to follow, just as Joshua's faith led him to advance, conquering Jericho and guiding the children of Israel toward the fulfillment of God's promise of Canaan.

True leaders must respond in the same way to achieve the promises God has set before them. Christian leaders must believe everything God has spoken and trust in the directives He gives. This belief and trust only become reality when a leader actively lives out the faith that God has bestowed upon them. The benefits of such faith, which knows no limitations, will enable the leader to achieve heights and accomplishments far beyond their own design or ability. And as this faith works through the leader, it is also imparted to those God has positioned to surround and follow them.

The boldness and drive that Christian leaders must possess stem from their faith in God. Faith is the channel through which God empowers leaders to embrace the objectives He has given. He speaks to us, and through our faith, we trust the directives He provides. Faith is the conception of what is possible before it is seen (Pringle, 2016). As leaders, Christ moves us by faith to inspire and guide others. Faith motivates our teammates, businesses, customers, churches, and those who follow us. From the examples of Abraham, Joshua, and our own leadership call, we see that God's purpose through faith is to lead us—and those connected to our leadership—toward a better future. Though the path is often unknown, sometimes risky, and frequently opposed, faith remains a powerful gift of the Holy Spirit. It guides Christian leaders to lead from their best selves, ultimately reaching the destination set by our leader, Jesus Christ (Blair, 2023).

FAITH APPLIED

When the faith "key" is applied to a Christian leader's approach, it brings various benefits that enhance the leader's effectiveness and deepen their success. Both the leader and those around them will witness a clear and growing display of:

Humility: Faith fosters humility within the Christian leader. The leader positions themselves in a posture where God is honored and recognized as sovereign. At the same time, they acknowledge themselves as the least in the Christ–follower dynamic. From this understanding flows a willingness to serve unselfishly. By modeling this attitude, the leader becomes an example to those they lead, helping others understand the posture they should take before God and encouraging them to embrace their role within the body of believers (Tweedt, 2019). Paul reminds believers:

For by the grace given me I say to every one of you: Do not think of yourself more highly than you ought, but rather think of yourself with sober judgment, in accordance with the faith God has distributed to each of you. *(Romans 12:3)*

Christian leaders must exhibit humility, inspired by God's undeserved outreach to them through Jesus' true love. Such humility calls for a continual denial of self, with a greater desire to recognize and exalt Christ.

Confidence: To many, faith is synonymous with confidence. In part, it is. However, faith is not confidence in itself—it is confidence in God. That faith in God, in turn, produces confidence within ourselves as we move in obedience to His commands. As we mature in our Christian walk, following God's direction becomes second nature. When obedience and compliance become the norm, a leader's perspective on missions, challenges, and realities is enriched by their deep trust in God.

Christian leaders often display a seemingly unexplainable confidence—an assurance that God works through what appears to be impossible. They respond less to what stands before them based on their own abilities and more on the principles, attributes, and tools God has given. Through His power, they understand that success is achievable. The writer of Hebrews reinforces this truth, stating:

"So do not throw away your confidence; it will be richly rewarded. You need to persevere so that when you have done the will of God, you will receive what he has promised." *(Hebrews 10:35–36, NIV)*

Christian leaders, through the key of faith, do not only demonstrate confidence for their own benefit. Their God-centered confidence flows outward, influencing those who follow them. It shapes the self-identity of others and furthers God's call to advance His Kingdom (Abel, 2011).

Inspiring Capabilities: Complacency is the enemy of progress in any area of life (WOL Ministries, 2022). At times, leaders are called to stabilize—to bring order where there is disorder. In such moments, Christian leaders are positioned by God, through the power of the Holy Spirit, to initiate a restructuring process. This process begins by placing God above the church, institution, or organization and making His will the primary focus.

From there, Christian leaders are driven by God's Spirit to guide whatever has been entrusted to them toward the goals the Lord has set.

While specific strategies are certainly necessary, the most essential requirement for advancement is for the leader to possess inspiring capabilities through faith. The ability to inspire is rarely acquired through a textbook formula or academic test. It is a sacred gift, given by the Holy Spirit, and birthed within a Christian leader because of their faith in Christ (Harmon, 2022).

This kind of faith is first recognized internally—when it drives, encourages, and shapes the leader's response to challenges. But it doesn't stay there. That same faith inspires those around them, motivating and empowering others to pursue the God-ordained achievements that lie ahead.

Consider the leadership of Joshua. When the time came to cross the Jordan, God said to him: "Be strong and courageous. Do not be afraid; for the Lord your God is with you wherever you go." *(Joshua 1:9, NIV)*

Joshua's faith in what God had spoken moved him forward.

His response inspired those around him to follow God's directive.

Their reply was:

"Whatever you have commanded us we will do, and wherever you send us we will go. Just as we fully obeyed Moses, so we will obey you. Only may the Lord your God be with you as he was with Moses. Whoever rebels against your word and does not obey it, whatever you may command them, will be put to death.

Only be strong and courageous!" *(Joshua 1:16–18, NIV)*

The faith key enables Christian leaders to inspire beyond limitations - even the limitations we set upon ourselves. Faith allows leaders to see further than the restrictions that threaten progress. While followers may not immediately see what the leader sees, it is the leader's faith-filled outlook that initiates and stirs the faith in others. Like Joshua, Moses, and Christ Himself, Christian leaders inspire others to move forward—toward what may only be faintly visible from a distance, but becomes clearer as they draw near.

That desire to "draw near" is almost always ignited by the leader, who models what it means to "walk by faith, not by sight" *(2 Corinthians 5:7, NIV)*.

SEVEN QUESTIONS TO ADVANCE THE UNDERSTANDING OF FAITH FOR CHRISTIAN LEADERSHIP SUCCESS

1. As a Christian leader, how would you personally define Faith?
2. In what way has faith impacted your journey as a Christian?
3. How is your faith demonstrated in your calling as a Christian leader?
4. In what way does faith influence your decision-making as a Christian leader?
5. How often is the need to utilize your faith "key" as a Christian leader?
6. Where do you see the connection between your faith and your ability as a Christian leader to inspire?
7. As a Christian Leader, in what ways would you teach the next generation of Christian leaders to utilize their faith to impact the next generation of Christ's followers?

Chapter Four
(Key Three)
Integrity

I didn't care too much about science. The experiments were cool, but when it came to charts, graphs, and tables, I checked out. So, when test time came—covering the many lessons our teacher had taught—most of the class and I were fully prepared to experience the backlash that came with bringing home an F.

One day, when it was time to take one of those tests, one of our classmates got hold of a cheat sheet that supposedly contained all the answers. He was generous with it as he made thirty photocopies in the library and handed them out to the entire class during lunch. When I say the whole class, I mean it—I got one too.

That evening, a sense of conviction settled in. I knew I wasn't ready for the test, and I was disappointed at the thought of possibly getting my first failing grade. But I also couldn't find peace in the idea of cheating. It wasn't the fear of getting caught. It was knowing that I wouldn't have earned the grade I'd receive. Because of that, I decided I'd rather fail honestly than pass dishonestly. So I ripped up the cheat sheet and threw it in the trash.

The next day came, and we all took the test. Most of the class finished in about twenty minutes, using the cheat sheet. I struggled through the full fifty-minute time limit, but I managed to complete it. Fully expecting to fail, I left the class, preparing myself for the backlash—from both the teacher and my mother. Meanwhile, most of the others celebrated, thinking they had gotten away with it and avoided the punishment that usually follows failure.

The following day, our teacher made an announcement. He said there were some students he was proud of and others he was disappointed in. Then he revealed that he knew about the cheat sheet—because he had created it. He explained that the answers on the sheet didn't match the test, as he had changed the entire test the night before. So, he knew exactly who had cheated and who had taken the test honestly.

Those who used the cheat sheet received a zero. Those who didn't were given an automatic score of one hundred. In addition, the students who cheated were assigned a week of detention, and the principal called home to alert their parents. Those who were honest were awarded something special: the integrity award, presented by the principal.

Out of all of us, twenty-seven classmates were ashamed because they had chosen to cheat. Only three of us were rewarded by the principal the following week. Our pictures were posted on the school bulletin board, and we got a month of free ice cream—which, back then, felt like gold.

It took that experience to teach me there's something truly valuable about doing things the right way. It's always tempting to take the easy path or go our own way. But when I held on to the principles my mother and other inspiring adults taught me—when I listened to my convictions—I stayed on the right side of a challenging situation. That's when I truly understood what integrity is all about: living by the standards you claim, even when it's hard.

Integrity helps a person maintain the identity they choose to reflect. When I first heard this, I thought the identity I was reflecting was my mom's. But over time, I came to understand that the image I was called to reflect was the image of God. If that was truly something I desired to do in the right way, integrity had to be a priority in my life. Just as integrity is essential for anyone following God, it is equally important for a Christian leader to possess and uphold it..

INTEGRITY DEFINED

Godly character is an essential component of a leader's life. Character serves as the guard of one's reputation. For anyone representing God, character is a necessity for success in all the callings they aim to fulfill. Without it, churches, organizations, and institutions across the world crumble into moral disarray. While character is crucial, there is one ingredient that aids in the formation and justification of good character: integrity (Davis, 2020).

The word *integrity*, derived from the Latin *integritas*, encompasses terms like wholeness, perfection, soundness, simplicity, completeness, and sincerity. Integrity is also the root word for *integer*, which refers to completeness or wholeness. This connects to Christians who possess integrity, as they have the internal components of being sound, reliable, trustworthy, and dependable (Kumi-Larbi, 2021).

Respected pastor and author Dr. David Jeremiah defines integrity for the Christian as: "When a person's words, actions, and values are aligned. The best way to become a leader worth following is to follow God, allowing Him to transform and direct us. He has infinite wisdom. As we attune and surrender ourselves to God, we grow in our ability to trust Him with ourselves, those we love, and those the Lord sends to follow us." *(Jeremiah, 2017)*

Many scholars and authors align with Jeremiah's view. Fapohunda defines integrity for Christians as behaviors and actions that are trustworthy, scriptural, charismatic, reliable, coherent, knowledgeable, and charitable (Fapohunda, 2021). Other definitions of integrity to consider include promise-keeping and demonstrating values through individual actions. Integrity focuses on keeping one's word, ensuring that one's actions align with their promises. For Christians, integrity means being honest and possessing strong moral principles. It also involves being whole and undivided—uncompromised, undefiled, unimpaired, and unwavering (Brown, 2014).

This writing will address integrity using the previously defined concepts, arriving at the following position: Christian integrity is the value of being truthful and living according to moral principles and uprightness. It is a disciplined, determined, and demonstrated behavior that serves as the established standard for the everyday life of a Christian, especially a Christian leader. As a noted portion of the identity of a Christian, integrity is visibly recognized as a leader's representation of Christ. It is demonstrated through their behavior and their response to the challenges that arise before them (Eruotor, 2022).

Integrity is core to a Christian leader's success. When leaders exercise their roles and operate with integrity, it motivates followers to do the same. Integrity becomes an influence that encourages others to live with integrity, as it paves the way for success and the development of those who echo the practices of their leaders (Clinton, 2012). Integrity is expected in situations that demand accountability and trust, especially in our relationships with others.

WHY INTEGRITY IS IMPERATIVE IN CHRISTIAN LEADERSHIP.

Jesus, the established example of integrity and the only person to demonstrate it perfectly, shows that integrity for Christian leadership is redemptive in its purposes. Leaders are called to embody the works and words of Jesus, reflecting His identity to those around them and to the world. They do this by demonstrating His life and moral identity through their own actions.

Unfortunately, as this writing will discuss, the absence of integrity creates a dysfunctional persona and a guilty conscience, where words and actions do not align. Followers of today's leaders often find themselves conflicted. When people act with integrity, the world may hate them as it did Christ, and society might even persecute them. However, leaders are called to demonstrate the reality of integrity, living with the peace of the Lord in their hearts and lives. Integrity culminates in the understanding that by remaining steadfast and unwavering, the name of Jesus will be glorified, vindicated, and worthy of the praise He deserves (Asamoah-Gyadu, 2024).

JOB

The Biblical story of Job is one that I often refer to individuals who are facing what seems to be unprovoked and unexplainable oppression. Job, like many believers around us, was righteous in a good way; he was "blameless and upright, he feared God and shunned evil" (Job 1:1, NIV).

Then, it seems as if "out of nowhere," Job—who was faithful to God—loses his family, his wealth, and his health in what appears to be an instant. However, this experience didn't come out of nowhere; Job's suffering was the result of a conversation between God and Satan. God allowed Satan to take away Job's wealth and children, and later, to afflict Job physically. Job grieved deeply, but he did not accuse God of wrongdoing.

It is hard to comprehend the scale of the calamity Job faced. Imagine being seen as faithful, living life not perfectly, but in a way that is recognized as pleasing to God. Job's life exemplified such righteousness as he was truly blessed by God. He had a family and children, and an abundance of fruit from the labor he performed.

Job's success was a result of God's hand upon Him. The Bible says, "God blessed the work of Job's hands, and his possessions increased in the land" (Job 1:10, NIV).

Job's recognition that everything he had was a gift from God is highlighted by his concern for his children. He worried that they might inadvertently offend God through their actions. So, Job, while maintaining his own righteousness, each morning sanctified them and offered burnt offerings on their behalf. (Job 1:5, NIV).

Despite petitioning God for forgiveness on behalf of his children, Job did not know that the suffering his family experienced was not due to their sin. Even when he lost everything—his wealth, his children, his health—Job did not cease from upholding his devotion to the Lord. He continued to claim God's righteousness above all else.

When everything fell apart for Job, there were additional contributing factors that, for the everyday person, would have been the reason for his spiritual disconnects. Among those witnessing these events and Job's suffering firsthand was his wife, who made her stance toward God clear. She suggested, through a question: "Do you still hold fast to your integrity? Curse God and die!" (Job 2:9, NIV). Despite the pressure, Job remained steadfast, allowing his integrity to reflect his position. He responded, "You speak as one of the foolish women speak. Shall we indeed accept good from God, and shall we not accept adversity? In all this, Job did not sin with his lips" (Job 2:10, NIV).

Job's three friends—Eliphaz, Bildad, and Zophar—arrived to comfort him, though their type of comfort was not what most would hope for. Initially, they appropriately mourned with him. However, they soon began offering multiple explanations for why these events were happening. These verbal offerings from his friends were filled with inaccuracies and underpinned by the belief that Job was suffering because of something he had done wrong. Consequently, they repeatedly encouraged Job to admit his wrongdoing and repent so that God would bless him again (Moore, 1983).

On one side, Job's wife presses him to curse God, die, and give up the righteous stance he's holding. On the other side, his three friends attempt to convince him that God is punishing him in response to his wrongdoings, thereby revealing the type of God he serves. Job was being attacked from both sides, all while facing the devastating reality of his circumstances. Imagine the distress of remaining strong in the moment, defending his belief in God despite the harsh words from those you love and respect (Kumi-Larbi, 2021). Though their words might not have seemed to be intentional, they sought to convince Job to defy God, given that it appeared God had denied and forgotten him.

Although Job didn't lead a church or an institution, he was a leader. Job held a sacred role, one that many believers currently occupy: he was a leader in his family. Throughout his time in this role, the one thing Job would not compromise was his integrity. He demonstrated that a truly blameless and upright person is so because of the Spirit, and not for personal gain or advantage they might receive from God (Hinks, 2000). He proved that "those who are righteous will continue in their ways, and those whose hands are clean from sin will grow stronger" (Job 17:9, NIV). Leaders like Job hold onto their integrity no matter the cost.

Christian leaders should embrace the example set by Job's experiences. Leaders will undoubtedly face hardships and moments of discouragement. They will encounter unexplained setbacks and peril, both in their leadership roles and personal lives. Especially in modern times, Christian leaders will face multiple disappointing outcomes. While these trials are difficult, leaders must understand that, like Job, God is fully aware of their situation. The period of oppression they experience is something God has allowed for a greater purpose. Knowing this should encourage leaders to hold on instead of letting go.

Job sets a clear standard for how leaders should respond to difficulties while maintaining their integrity. He did not reject God. He did not accept the notion of a God-given curse, nor did he entertain the alternative of wishing for death (Moore, 1983). In other words, Job did not let his circumstances serve as an excuse to push God away or attempt to take matters into his own hands by doing what only God could do. Integrity, which means being unwavering and uncompromising in one's identity, prevents the leader from compromising their values, even in moments of temporary adversity. These moments may have long-lasting consequences if they cause a leader to abandon who they are in Christ (Kang-Kul Cho, 2014).

Leaders are called to endure adversity because their leadership—whether over a church, institution, or family—requires it. Job reminds us that despite life's setbacks, integrity is an essential part of being a believer in God, and even more so, an effective Christian leader.

WHY INTEGRITY IS IMPORTANT TO CHRISTIAN LEADERSHIP

When I first made a serious investment in studying the Biblical book of Job, two critical insights resonated with me—insights that I had not fully grasped when I merely skimmed through it. First, Job was a sinner. Though he was considered righteous, he was not without flaws. He was imperfect and occasionally fell short. Through his story, I saw that Job was led to repent, not just once, but repeatedly, for various iniquities. This repeated repentance highlighted his deep desire to maintain a strong connection with God. It also explains why Job took the extraordinary step of repenting for his children, recognizing that their actions reflected upon him as their father. He felt responsible for who they were and what they might become.

What better example of leadership can we find than Job's acts and beliefs?

Another key point about Job is that he was a man who truly feared God. The fear of God is not about seeing the Lord as a spooky being or intimidating presence. To fear God means to have a deep reverence for Him, recognizing that He knows all and has complete control over everything. God's power and presence are limitless, and our understanding of Him is always limited. This realization naturally leads to awe and respect for the Lord. This sacred relationship is precious to those who truly fear Him. God, as the sovereign controller of all, is integral to the functioning of any leader. Leaders are called to revere God as Job did, understanding the purpose of this reverence and how it relates to integrity. The fear of God, as experienced by true believers, becomes a vital aspect of the integrity that God empowers in those who are called to lead, especially when leadership challenges arise (Brodie, 2024).

There is nothing that strengthens integrity like a deep reverence for the sovereign Judge of the universe. The greatest leader, Jesus, exemplifies this integrity. As recorded in both Matthew and Luke, after His baptism, Jesus is led by the Holy Spirit into the wilderness, where He is tempted by Satan. It is crucial to understand from the outset that our integrity as leaders can only be compromised by Satan and his schemes when we fail to let our integrity be defined by who we are in Christ.

Jesus experienced this when Satan approached Him in a state of extreme physical and emotional vulnerability—fatigued, weakened, starved, and disoriented after forty days of fasting in the heat of the wilderness, in obedience to God. Satan came offering not only what Jesus physically needed but also what, from a human perspective, would be most tempting and desirable. In three distinct attempts, Satan tried to provoke Jesus to abandon His divine mission and prioritize personal gratification. But each time, Jesus stood firm, responding with unwavering faith by declaring, "It is written." He quoted Scripture to reject every deceptive invitation to sin (Luke 4:1–13, NIV). What's most powerful about this exchange is that, although Jesus was in a compromised physical state, He never compromised spiritually. The temptations were real, and Satan's offers could have ended His immediate suffering—yet they were not enough to make Him sacrifice His integrity. For Jesus, nothing was worth walking away from the will of His Father.

What stands out in these exchanges is that although Jesus was in a physically compromised state, He never compromised His integrity. Even though the temptation was real and Satan's offers could have ended His suffering, they were not enough to make Him forfeit His commitment to His Father. For Jesus, nothing was worth walking away from His Father's will.

Consider the keys presented thus far. Through the Holy Spirit, our key ring now includes prayer and faith. Each of these keys coexists in harmony. We pray because we recognize our need to communicate with God, and we believe that God will deliver because of the faith we have in Him. We remain steadfast in both prayer and faith because of the integrity demonstrated by Jesus, and because God has given each leader the gift of integrity. Integrity is sacred, and it is a quality that leaders must hold onto, as it operates fluidly and creates effective leadership when used alongside all the other keys.

Integrity not only stabilizes leaders in challenging moments, but it is also a crucial part of continuous Christian leadership development. Integrity flows from a deep, personal walk with God and a commitment to live out the life of Christ daily. It is both a character trait and a practical discipline. Talent, success, and leadership skills are insufficient without personal integrity (White, 2009). This is why Jesus Himself calls leaders to integrity—because those who lead in faith must be true to their word, reflecting their faith in Him. Integrity reminds us of to whom we belong, whom we report to, and how we live.

Leaders have a responsibility to reflect, in our actions, words, and decisions, the true identity of a Christian leader, which is ultimately the identity of Christ Himself. It is imperative that we take seriously the calling to lead the body of Christ. Our character and behavior should reflect Him and His calling to the best of our abilities. Leaders must prioritize demonstrating integrity by following through on what we say and acting in accordance with what we believe (Krejcir, 2006). When integrity is neglected or taken for granted, we risk becoming frauds. Our lack of integrity not only negatively impacts us individually; it undermines the entire character, function, and trust of the body of Christ. A lack of integrity leads to leadership dysfunction and ineffectiveness.

UNAPPLIED INTEGRITY

Integrity for the Christian leader is demonstrated through their sincere desire to fully comply with the will of God. It involves leaders having a deep understanding of God's word, recognizing what He calls for, and being receptive to walking in His ways (Winston, 2018). Since God's word is foundational to integrity, it places emphasis on the importance of leaders keeping their word. What they speak must align with their actions. This means keeping promises and living out the same values they advocate for (Brown, 2014).

Unfortunately, a lack of applied integrity is all too common in Christian leadership. This failure has led to the downfall of many ministries and the failure of numerous Christian leaders. The absence of integrity is often linked to "moral uprightness," a term associated with unfulfilled integrity. This behavior, sadly, has become an unfortunate expectation in some circles of Christian leadership. Such failures can result in sexual misconduct, misappropriation of funds, greed, a love of money, personal moral failures, and overall leadership incompetence.

Integrity, empowered by the Holy Spirit, forms a protective structure for Christian leaders, preventing worldly, unspiritual approaches from infiltrating their leadership. When truth-telling is emphasized and aligned with the righteousness of God (Winston, 2018), falsehoods and improper leadership behaviors are less likely to compromise the Christian way of leadership. Instead, integrity-driven leadership is rooted in God's established Biblical principles.

A failure in integrity is often recognized when leaders attempt to merge cultural trends with Christianity. For instance, in recent years, many leaders have adopted lifestyles and behaviors that closely mirror secular celebrities or individuals who gain fame through unbiblical means. Popularity often leads Christian leaders to compromise integrity, trading the desire to represent Christ for the approval of the world. This results in a lack of holiness in their approach, an unhealthy obsession with worldly practices, and the influence of secular culture in shaping their decisions and actions. This worldly influence diminishes their commitment to God's commandments, often leading to obvious deficiencies in their leadership.

A key component of integrity is trust, and it is clear that distrust in leadership signals a breakdown in integrity. Gallup's 2023 Honesty and Ethics poll highlights this, showing that 34% of churchgoers believe pastors who once had high levels of honesty and ethics no longer do. This decline in trust has led to a drop in the perception of trustworthy leaders, with less than one-third of Americans rating pastors highly for honesty and ethics— the lowest point in Gallup's survey history. Additionally, only 45% of respondents believe pastors maintain average honesty and ethical standards, while 1 in 5 (20%) rate these standards as low or very low (Earls, 2024a).

Why are leaders distrusted? Over the last sixty years, numerous reports and scandals have surfaced concerning Christian leaders. The 1980s were marked by investigations into popular television evangelists who were scrutinized by governmental authorities for financial mishandling and excessive spending, often reflected in their lavish lifestyles.

In the following decade, the trust in Christian leaders continued to erode, as sexual misconduct, extramarital affairs, interactions with prostitutes, and blatant sexual sin—including involvement in fornication and homosexual group gatherings—became weekly headlines. As the new millennium dawned, reports of child sex abuse scandals involving Roman Catholic priests, alongside subsequent cover-ups, became an all too common story. These scandals deeply grieved believers and fueled the claims of atheists who said, "They knew it all along" (Effron, 2019).

The lack of integrity among Christian leaders is not just a domestic issue; it is international as well. While the underlying reasons for this erosion of trust are similar globally, the severity of the problem varies by region. In Ghana, for instance, where Christianity has seen substantial growth, the compromised integrity of Christian leaders is a pressing concern. Like many of their American counterparts, some Christian leaders in Ghana enter leadership roles for personal gain. These leaders are often entangled in corruption, bribery, embezzlement, fraud, favoritism, extortion, illicit contributions, nepotism, and abuse of power (Kumi-Larbi, 2021). This behavior is frequently intertwined with government corruption, further compromising the sanctity of the church. Tragically, this has become so commonplace in Ghana that the next generation of leaders anticipates participation in such unethical behaviors. Congregants, many of whom are learning the difference between honest and dishonest practices, are left conflicted and disillusioned.

The nation of Kenya is also facing similar challenges. Often described as plagued by "bad leadership," Christian leaders in Kenya have been accused of exchanging their moral integrity for kickbacks and cooperation in unethical dealings. These leaders have been known to act as brokers for politicians, accepting cash payouts or offering "religious support" in return for their assistance. Such actions by both government and Christian leaders have fostered widespread resentment toward Christianity among the local population. The same leaders who once championed righteousness have now become a source of disillusionment for many Kenyans who longed to follow leaders who were supposed to embody Christ's example (Wainaina, 2023).

Trust is essential for Christian leaders. These leaders are called to share and demonstrate truth, but without trust, the truth they aim to convey is often not received. While the message itself can be rejected, the reception of truth is largely influenced by the messenger. If the messenger is compromised, the truth is likely to go unheard. Trust allows for truth to be shared, as the act of transmission requires vulnerability. When a listener does not allow themselves to be vulnerable, it is often because they are uncomfortable with the person delivering the message. This discomfort frequently stems from a lack of trust in the messenger, which is often rooted in a lack of integrity (Hull, 2006).

Leaders may proclaim, "This should be," but if it is not true in their own lives, the listeners will sense hypocrisy, which leads to the dismissal of the message. Christian leaders are meant to leave a lasting impression that shapes lives. However, they cannot offer guidance, prescriptions for improvement, or calls for change unless they are willing to live by their own teachings. How can a Christian leader speak life into a sinner if their own life is defined by sin? This is why trust is crucial for Christian leaders. Trust is earned when a leader demonstrates integrity, as it shows they can be relied upon to live according to the very principles they encourage others to follow. Leaders who exhibit integrity inspire confidence because they model what they preach and live by the truth they share (Northouse, 2022).

INTEGRITY APPLIED

When integrity becomes a priority and a defining characteristic of the Christian leader, it showcases individual ethics and sets a standard not only for the leader but also for those who follow them. Integrity enables the Christian leader to listen to and consider the perspectives of others, ensuring that decisions are made with care and contribute to building positive, ethical cultures (Chabot, 2023). Integrity also motivates followers to cooperate toward shared goals. People connect not just to the leader's words, but to the way the leader behaves. This highlights how integrity creates a strong bond between leaders and their followers, as it establishes the leader as an honest, reliable, and responsible individual who upholds a standard for themselves and encourages others to do the same, following the biblical principles set by Christ. Furthermore, when leadership integrity is demonstrated, it influences parishioners in church settings or colleagues in business, inspiring a commitment to personal growth and development. This, in turn, leads to the achievement of what once seemed impossible and paves the way for the creation of future leaders who understand the vital importance of prioritizing integrity (Eruotor, 2022).

Leaders with integrity are highly regarded and respected because they remain the same person regardless of the environment or role they are in. They operate out of the same values and worldview, whether in personal, professional, or ministry settings (Rapp, 2021). The integrity they hold onto prevents them from changing into someone who acts inconsistently or contrary to their principles. Instead, they are firmly committed to being defined by their Lord, Jesus Christ. Christian leaders are not only obligated but also honored to serve as models for others. However, it is important to note that their aim is not to model sinful behaviors, but rather the example of the Savior. Even in times of failure, integrity compels them to repent, and public repentance, if necessary, serves as a powerful testimony of how someone, in a moment of weakness, can realign themselves with Christ. Integrity is the overarching principle that guides their life. Christian leaders are called to be living examples of how to walk according to God's will. Their leadership cannot be limited to words alone; their actions must align with their speech, fostering a culture of transparency and authenticity (Ottestad, 2023). Scripture reminds both leaders and believers that "whoever walks in integrity walks securely, but whoever takes crooked paths will be found out" (Proverbs 10:9, NIV). Integrity does not just make a leader good—it empowers them to be effective in fulfilling their calling.

Seven Questions to Advance the Understanding of Integrity for Christian Leadership Success

1. How do you define integrity as a Christian leader?
2. Do you hold yourself accountable to someone for your leadership decisions?
3. If someone under your leadership branch did not understand the value of integrity, what three things would you offer to them to help them grasp integrity's importance?
4. How would you address an individual under your leadership who was not operating within the confines of the integrity they stated that defined them?
5. As a Christian leader, does your personal life align with the values you preach to others? What methods do you employ to establish this symmetry?
6. Where, in your opinion, do integrity and repentance align?
7. Describe a moment as a Christian Leader where your integrity led you to make an unpopular but righteous-based decision that impacted multiple members of your organization.

CHAPTER FIVE
(KEY FOUR) VISION

Two years into establishing the Bible study I mentioned earlier, attendance was growing, and scriptural knowledge was increasing—not only for the participants but also for me. Preparing for and conducting the weekly gatherings became a source of joy. It was something I looked forward to, sensing a profound inner transformation taking place within me. I was falling more and more in love with the Word of God, experiencing Him in ways I never had before. Equally exciting was the newfound enthusiasm I felt for sharing His Word. I began to recognize a God given ability to teach and help my friends better understand what Scripture means, how it applies to who we are now, and what we are all called to do and be.

My submission to God's directives regarding the Bible study—though a tough lesson in humility—was leading me to a level of Christianity I had never experienced before. God began revealing things to me, and I found myself discerning more clearly the reasons behind many of His directives. Much of it centered around trust: the more I trusted, the more He allowed me to see. Then, one significant evening after a Wednesday night Prayer and Bible fellowship, something happened that opened my eyes to something I had never imagined.

After the final "God bless you" was extended to a departing Bible study guest, I sat down and thanked Jesus for allowing the lesson to go smoothly and for choosing me to be a contributor to His kingdom. That night, I was deeply moved with gratitude, genuinely sensing that my obedient service to Christ earned a "well done" status. As I stood up and motioned to gather my things to leave, an image overwhelmed me, obscuring my view of the adjacent counter. I wasn't blind, but my vision was distorted, and the confusion made me close my eyes. As I did, I saw something that seemed so realistic and futuristic that I was dumbfounded.

I found myself standing in front of a group of people—maybe fifty to eighty in attendance—listening intently to a Biblical lesson I was teaching. The setting wasn't a store, but it wasn't a traditional church either. It resembled a large, modern room equipped with various technical devices: cameras, lights, microphones, and computers.

I saw a young woman silently operating and directing the flow of the lesson, ensuring nothing disturbed what was happening. The audience's enthusiasm was palpable as they were engaged and excited by God's Word. Behind the scenes, I saw a support team— a group of individuals who shared that agreed with the directive God commanded of us, who prioritized His people, walking with them in faith as new disciples. Collectively, what O captured from what I saw was clear: God was preparing for us to establish a place where His Word could be read, taught, explained, and applied to the lives of those He had redeemed. I was to play a significant role in this vision. Through sacrifice, many lives would be touched and transformed. The focus was God's Word; the objective was to teach and extend it effectively. The place would be devoted to Him—not to men or the ideals of the world. What God showed me that day was more than just a glimpse; it was a vision of what would later become the house of prayer I would pastor and lead: Restoration Church.

Because I had submitted my life to God, He graciously afforded to me the opportunity to witness the future He had in store for me. At that time, I had never considered a future involving church leadership, being a Bible teacher, or even becoming a pastor. But when God revealed what was to come, I believed it wholeheartedly and accepted what He showed me. This vision stood in stark contrast to much of what I had experienced at church previously. What I was shown was different from the prophetic words I was given, and the opinions of so many people concerning my future. I was confident that this vision was from God, showing me exactly how my God-given time in this world would be spent.

I recalled the moment when the Holy Spirit was poured out on those who believed in God's word, as prophesied by Joel: "I will pour out my Spirit on all people. Your sons and daughters will prophesy, your old men will dream dreams, your young men will see visions" (Joel 2:28, NIV). At that time, as a "young man," the vision God provided only deepened my sense of calling and the purpose He had placed before me. Through this vision, I saw how God would continually humble me and use me to bring more people into His kingdom.

VISION DEFINED

The topic of visions—particularly within the prophetic context— can be a sensitive one among Christians. This sensitivity often stems from confusion between visions and dreams, as well as from the frequent mishandling or vague interpretation of visions. Not every mental image is a God-given vision, nor does every thought, whether it arises during rest or full consciousness, qualify as such. While many believers may intellectually grasp this distinction, the concept of vision remains widely misunderstood. Nevertheless, it is a vital gift from God—one that He expects believers and leaders to recognize, steward, and apply with discernment.

To ensure clarity and alignment with the key concepts presented in this writing, it's essential to define what a vision truly is. According to Vines, vision is a prophetic image granted by God, through which divine revelation is disclosed. The Hebrew term *chizzayon* further supports this understanding, as it translates to "divine communication" (Strongs, 1798). A prime example of this is the vision God granted to the prophet Nathan regarding King David. This vision foretold the future of Israel, focusing on David's son, who would one day rule the nation, establish a reign founded on God's grace and protection, and be tasked with building a temple in honor of God's name (2 Samuel 7:12-17, NIV). Through this vision, God revealed the future of both His chosen king and His kingdom.

Vision is derived from the Greek term *horama*, meaning "that which is seen" or "an appearance" (Strongs, 1798). Barna defines vision as a clear mental image of a preferable future, one that is divinely inspired and given to God's chosen servants. This vision is rooted in a true understanding of God, self, and the circumstances at hand (Barton, 2022). According to the *Evangelical Dictionary of Biblical Theology*, visions serve as a means of communication between a heavenly being—such as God, Jesus, the Holy Spirit, or angels—and an earthly recipient (Rollins, 2020).

In *Future-Focused Leadership*, vision is presented as a fundamental human emotion that a leader strives to experience with those they lead. It serves to center the group, enabling them to make a lasting, existential impact on the world (Petty, 2022). When integrated with Pastor and author Charles Stanley's perspective, vision emerges as a vivid mental picture of what could be, driven by the deep conviction that it should be. Stanley further emphasizes that vision carries a moral element, compelling a sense of urgency (Ministries, 2020).

Vision stands apart from the other keys previously discussed and those that will be covered later. A God-given vision is focused on the future—not just for ourselves, but for those we serve and the institutions we represent. In this vision, God highlights a problem, offers a solution, and prompts action from others. The arrival and use of visions are significant because an individual cannot control when or how they will receive this gift. Vision is a divine attribute, one that can only be granted by God for purposes He deems fit (Henson, 2018).

However, while Christians cannot control the vision itself, they can pray for God's guidance, seeking confirmation and clarity on specific matters. A leader can also strive to be open to divine inspiration, so that they, in turn, can inspire others to follow what God has revealed about the future according to His will.

Leaders who are commissioned by God are often entrusted with the "key" of vision. This key allows them to form a plan for the future and inspire others to embrace it. Consider the example of Nehemiah.

Deeply saddened by the devastation of Jerusalem, Nehemiah prayed to God, and in response, God gave him a vision of restoration. This vision began with the rebuilding of the city's walls. Although the task seemed straightforward, it was far from simple. The destruction of Jerusalem was so extensive that the idea of restoration seemed nearly impossible (Neh. 2:11-18, NIV).

Vision stands apart from the other keys previously discussed and those that will be covered later. A God-given vision is focused on the future—not just for ourselves, but for those we serve and the institutions we represent. In this vision, God highlights a problem, offers a solution, and prompts action from others. The arrival and use of visions are significant because an individual cannot control when or how they will receive this gift. Vision is a divine attribute, one that can only be granted by God for purposes He deems fit (Henson, 2018).

However, while Christians cannot control the vision itself, they can pray for God's guidance, seeking confirmation and clarity on specific matters. A leader can also strive to be open to divine inspiration, so that they, in turn, can inspire others to follow what God has revealed about the future according to His will.

Leaders who are commissioned by God are often entrusted with the "key" of vision. This key allows them to form a plan for the future and inspire others to embrace it. Consider the example of Nehemiah. Deeply saddened by the devastation of Jerusalem, Nehemiah prayed to God, and in response, God gave him a vision of restoration. This vision began with the rebuilding of the city's walls. Although the task seemed straightforward, it was far from simple. The destruction of Jerusalem was so extensive that the idea of restoration seemed nearly impossible (Neh. 2:11-18, NIV).

Once again, the Christian leader must hold the vision key. In other words, leaders of God's people must be visionaries— those who have a clear and compelling vision from God for their ministries. They must not only be able to articulate that vision but also advocate for it, inspiring and persuading others to join in making it a reality (Barton, 2022). The vision that God imparts to leaders shapes the direction of their leadership, and it is God's calling that determines the path the Christian leader will follow to bring that vision to life.

PETER

Many Bible readers may question whether the disciple Peter was suited for a leadership role. This doubt becomes clearer after Jesus' prophecy is fulfilled, with Peter denying Him three times. After such a misstep, who would have thought Peter would be fit for leadership? The answer is Jesus. From the very beginning, Jesus made it clear regarding Peter, saying, "You are Peter, and on this rock I will build my church, and the gates of hell shall not prevail against it" (Matt. 16:18, NIV). In this statement, Jesus wasn't declaring that the church would be built upon Peter, but rather, Jesus was using a play on words to illustrate that Peter would play a significant role in the church's foundation.

Peter's name means "rock," and since Jesus intended to build His church on a rock, it suggests that Peter would play a significant role in the church's foundation. This becomes evident, along with Peter's leadership role, when Jesus calls him first to proclaim the gospel to the Gentiles.

Initially, Peter was called to Joppa to assist with the restoration of a disciple named Tabitha, who had fallen ill and died. After Peter prayed, she was miraculously healed, and he stayed in Joppa at the house of Simon the Tanner. While there, Peter went to the rooftop and fell into a trance. He saw heaven open, and a large sheet, bound at the four corners, descended to him, bringing with it all kinds of four-footed animals, wild beasts, creeping things, and birds of the air. Then a voice spoke, saying, "Rise, Peter, kill and eat." Peter, however, was reluctant, as his culture and religion forbade him from consuming such animals, considering them unclean. But the Lord responded, making it clear: "What God has cleansed, you must not call common" (Acts 10:10-16, NIV). While the objects in the vision were animals, the lesson was not about the consumption of different animal meats. It was about the relationship between Jews and Gentiles. Jesus was teaching Peter that just as Jews are cleansed by faith, so too are the Gentiles. They, too, are worthy of the saving grace of the Gospel.

Peter followed God's command and traveled with three men sent by Cornelius, a Roman centurion from Caesarea who was a devout worshiper of God. The Holy Spirit had compelled Peter to join them, and at the same time, God sent His angel to Cornelius, instructing him to find Peter and deliver a message. As Peter entered Cornelius's house, he reminded him that, according to Jewish law, it was forbidden for Jews to associate with Gentiles. However, Peter explained how God had shown him in a vision not to call anyone common or unclean. Peter understood that the animals in his vision were symbolic of the Gentiles, whom God was preparing to hear the gospel. Cornelius then shared his experience of the angel who had instructed him to seek out Peter, and both men realized that God had orchestrated their meeting.

Peter preached the gospel to everyone gathered at Cornelius's house, and as he spoke, the Gentiles received the Holy Spirit and were baptized. This moment marked the beginning of a divine expansion— revealing that the gospel was meant for all people, not just the Jews (Acts 10:34–43, NIV). It was through Peter's obedience to God's vision showed him that salvation was extended to the Gentiles. These visions serve to bring more people to Christ, especially those who are far off or facing blinding challenges that create a wedge between themselves and the salvific reality of Christ.

Just as God used visions to reveal His will to Peter, He continues to give visions to Christian leaders for various purposes. These visions serve to bring more people to Christ, especially those who are far off. Ultimately, these visions lead to the revelation of God's glory, giving leaders the foresight to prepare for His will to manifest in the world.

Why Vision is Important to Christian Leadership

Through a vision, God revealed His plan for the faith to Peter—not just so he would understand, but so that Peter could see his role in God's work and how it would impact all people, including the least of these. This is the purpose of visions: God gives leaders a picture, or an understanding, of what He is doing, what will take place, and why what He is revealing will benefit those He loves. Such a vision provides Christian leaders with the stability they need, but also encourages the reliability they must have toward God, who is directing their steps.

For Christian leaders, vision is a vital outlook that originates from within and guides their actions. When God plants a vision in a leader, it stirs a desire for growth and improvement. This is why, when a vision exists, the hopes and ideals that define the leader are also realized—because those hopes and ideals are rooted in God's will. Understanding that their vision is God-ordained gives leaders a sense of purpose, motivating them to press forward, deny themselves, and serve selflessly those they are called to lead (Bechervaise, 2013). Therefore, vision is more than a dream or a mere glimpse of the future. Those called by God to lead must discern whether a vision is truly from God.

Christian leaders are not meant to create their own agendas.

Those called by God to lead must discern of a vision is truly from God. Saul of Tarsus, as a leader within the Pharisees, followed a cultural agenda that was not aligned with God's plan for the future. Saul's agenda was to eradicate Christianity, while God's agenda was to convert nonbelievers to believers in Christ. Saul could not see this at the time, which is why God had to transform his understanding— Paul had an unclear view not only about those following the way, but also how He saw the Lord.

This is the challenge many leaders face today. A vision exists, but a crucial question must always be answered: Is this vision from God, and does it lead to the fulfillment of His calling? For Saul and many others, the barrier is their own perception of what God wants or the future image they envision for society. In many cases, these visions are not from God, as they do not result in His glorification. Most are the thoughts of mankind, reflecting what the Lord spoke through Isaiah: "For my thoughts are not your thoughts, neither are your ways my ways," declares the LORD (Isaiah 55:8, NIV).

Simply put, when God gives a vision, it reveals what God wants, when He wants it done, and what He wants us to be excited about. In essence, this vision is given to inspire enthusiasm as we are shown what God has planned for us to see and experience. When leaders receive this vision and gain an understanding of it, their motivation to advance is driven by a desire to honor God. This understanding begins with the leader seeing and believing what is possible, then communicating through faith and with courage what can be, should be, and will be. A leader who is called by God and can effectively translate that vision is a leader who motivates others. When communicated with excellence, the vision associated with God's call inspires others to embrace the challenge of great work and the effective service of those within the Kingdom of God and those called to receive salvation in Jesus Christ (Ayers, 2021).

Consider Dr. Martin Luther King Jr.'s "I Have a Dream" speech. The speech was centered on the values of equality and how they would foster unity in America. It was a calling by God that kept him focused on the future God desires for us (Garrow, 2004). To this day, the world continues to strive toward that dream. The reason for this is that people believed in the vision Dr. King communicated, seeing it as from God, and recognized that the destination was worth pursuing. We continue to see progress toward Dr. King's dream, and with each passing day, the vision he received from God continues to unfold. As a society, we are blessed that Dr. King responded to the vision God gave him, as we witness the world moving closer to seeing that dream fulfilled.

Just as it was for Dr. King, vision is a vital key for Christian leaders, and it can only be effectively utilized when the vision originates from God. For leaders, vision is a picture of a better future—for their groups or for individuals they are working with. Discernment is crucial when it comes to visions, as authentic visions are informed by the principles of Scripture and, at times, supplemented by direct communication from God. In other words, we can know in general what God desires for the church, as well as Christian organizations and institutions, because the Bible reveals God's will. However, God often provides a unique application of that direction, tailored to specific local conditions and personalities. Once again, discernment plays a key role in properly conceptualizing visions. Leaders should continually seek these supplemental insights through prayer and reflection.

Overall, the vision given to Christian leaders by God provides a spiritual roadmap to guide their congregations, as well as members of organizations and institutions, toward spiritual growth. It motivates and challenges followers to invest themselves in the future that God has set before them. This is only possible through faith, and the vision must first be exemplified by the leader. This is how believers move forward, advance in growth, and become who God has called them to be. Vision is something shared—it is initially experienced by the leader but is then extended to their followers (McCallum, 2024). Without vision, the leader is, in a sense, walking alone, disconnected, which results in followers feeling a lack of progress.

When leaders receive and embrace vision as Christian overseers, it's about fostering an environment that encourages transformation. Vision ignites passion, unites individuals with a shared purpose, and paves the way for faithful followers to make a significant impact (Rodecap, 2023). Vision brings about change in the lives of those who embrace it, both within the Christian community and in the surrounding society. When allowed to take root, vision becomes a powerful catalyst for transformation, making it a key tool in a Christian leader's effectiveness.

VISION APPLIED

The goal here is not to belabor the point, but it's important to stress how essential it is for Christian leaders to understand this premise: Vision is not something self-conceived by the leader. Vision for the Christian leader originates from God and is a gift given to them. This vision must always remain subject to God's guidance and be open to prayerful reconsideration. The vision is designed to fulfill God's purpose, so the leader delivering it should always see themselves as a servant (Nichols, 2010). Unfortunately, many leaders lack discernment and struggle to distinguish between what God is showing them regarding their mission and what they personally desire for their ministry. These are two different perspectives that are often merged, leading to the failure and distress that this writing seeks to avoid (McCallum, 2024). When vision is properly connected to the previously discussed keys - prayer, faith, integrity, all empowered by the Holy Spirit - it leads to the benefits outlined below.

1. When applied, vision gives the Christian leader divine direction.

A leader must be going in the right direction, and vision is not merely a suggestion or a vague idea—it is a directive from God. Vision is divine guidance, gifted to the Christian leader, that continuously advocates for the leader to stay on the path God has set. This ensures that the leader's journey aligns with God's will, so the mission will culminate in the fulfillment of the image the leader was shown and what God has designated.

For example, Moses was told that the ultimate goal of leading the Hebrews out of Egypt was to reach the Promised Land. However, there was a shorter route from Egypt to Canaan. God chose to lead Moses and the Israelites through the desert, with the Red Sea as a boundary. It was through God's divine direction that Moses took this longer, seemingly more difficult route. This journey allowed God's power to be revealed when the Red Sea parted, and the pursuing Egyptian army was drowned as the waters closed in on them. Vision, therefore, is not just about reaching the finish line; it is God giving divine direction so that the Christian leader, guided by the Holy Spirit, can discern the right paths to take throughout the journey.

2. When applied, vision gives the Christian leader endurance.

Do we remember why God allowed Moses to send the twelve spies into Canaan—the land He had promised to Abraham? He wanted His people to catch a glimpse of what was to come to stir their excitement and build anticipation for everything to come that He had prepared for them. Despite ten of the tribal leaders returning with fear-driven, negative reports, two stood firm in their faith, affirming God's plan. Caleb and Joshua's report was clear and full of confidence:

"The land which we passed through to spy out is an exceedingly good land. If the Lord is pleased with us, then He will bring us into this land and give it to us, a land which flows with milk and honey. Only do not rebel against the Lord; and do not fear the people of the land, for they will be our prey. Their protection is gone from them, and the Lord is with us; do not fear them." (Num. 14:7–9, NIV)

Though there were real obstacles standing between the

people and the land, God allowed them to see it so they could begin to envision what was possible. Caleb and Joshua aligned their perspective with what God had shown, rather than what fear and emotion tried to convince them was impossible. Their vision, shaped by faith, motivated them to believe.

In the same way, vision gives the Christian leader the strength to press forward. As Paul wrote, we must strive "toward the goal to win the prize for which God has called me heavenward in Christ Jesus" (Phil. 3:13–14, NIV).

As leaders, we will face countless reasons to quit, to resign, or to give up. But when God paints a picture in our minds—a vision of success, of victory, of overcoming the odds—it instills endurance. That divine image fuels our determination until what God has drawn in the heart and mind of the Christian leader becomes reality.

3. When applied, vision gives the Christian leader their purpose.

Some might say that vision gives leaders their goal—and to an extent, this is true. But that perspective is incomplete. Vision doesn't stop at defining a specific goal; it goes further by shaping and evaluating a leader's purpose. Vision is a meaningful image of the future that connects to a leader's sense of calling and draws forth their full commitment and energy (Barton, 1997).

When vision is given by God, it helps leaders understand not only what they are called to do or where they are to go, but also who they are called to become. Vision reveals more than an external objective—it offers a glimpse into how God sees the leader. This vision becomes a mirror through which internal development begins.

It's through this divine insight that spiritual growth and maturation willingly unfold. Leaders begin to understand the deeper reason for their calling, and with self-initiated humility, they surrender their leadership to God's dominion. Through this process, they are transformed. By the time the mission is fulfilled, they are no longer the same individuals who first received the assignment. Vision, therefore, doesn't just propel a leader forward—it changes them in the process.

A relatable example of such a leader is found in a humble man named Joseph, who cared deeply about obeying God. Joseph was pledged to marry a young woman named Mary, only to discover that she was pregnant—and not by him. After an angel of the Lord appeared to him and explained that Mary was pregnant through the Holy Spirit, Joseph was encouraged not to be afraid to take her as his wife. Though he initially hesitated, he soon obeyed.

Joseph seemed to grasp the reason God had placed him in such an unconventional situation. God was fulfilling His promise to the world through this woman who would become Joseph's wife. Though God was the heavenly Father of the child, Jesus would still need an earthly father. Joseph was called to fill that role, to honor that calling, and to lead Mary and Jesus as his family (Romer & Ruckl, 2009). Fatherhood would be Joseph's purpose.

Joseph demonstrated his understanding of this divine leadership role when he chose not to consummate the marriage until after Jesus was born (Matthew 1:25, NIV), thereby protecting the integrity of the virgin birth. Following Caesar's decree, Joseph took Mary to Bethlehem to be registered for the census, as required, because it was the town of his ancestors (Luke 2:4–5, NIV). Then, forty days after Jesus' birth, Joseph brought Mary and the infant Jesus to Jerusalem to dedicate Him at the temple, in accordance with the Law of Moses (Luke 2:22–24, NIV). Each of these actions fulfilled what had been prophesied, confirming the divine arrival of the Messiah.

Like Joseph, leaders are called to protect, influence, and guide others toward the destinations that God establishes.

It is believed that the Holy Spirit, in His communication with Joseph, clearly revealed His intentions for Mary and the child she carried (Romer & Ruckl, 2009). In simple terms, the Holy Spirit painted a vision for Joseph—making clear the objective and Joseph's part in it as the leader of this extraordinary family. And because Joseph saw the vision, believed in it, and accepted it, he responded faithfully. Through this vision, Joseph discovered his purpose and stepped into one of the most quietly powerful examples of leadership found in Scripture.

4. When applied, vision aids the Christian leader in forming future Christian leaders.

When Christian leaders faithfully follow the vision God has given them, their followers are given a clear example of what it looks like to follow God. While this might sound complex, within the scope of a leader's influence, a powerful truth unfolds: when a leader shares what God has revealed and nurtures excitement among their people, somewhere within that group, the beginnings of another leader are being formed. That individual becomes more open and receptive to the visions God will give concerning their own future.

Many researchers agree that vision is one of the most essential qualities of influential leaders—on par with the ability to communicate clearly and build trust. A leader's decisions and strategies often reflect their perception of what a movement can become and how God is shaping its direction. A strong leader builds trust in the vision by living it out consistently and demonstrating what it takes to bring it to fruition.

This consistency and authenticity become a spark—one that inspires others to desire their own encounters with God. In witnessing a leader pursue God's agenda, others begin to long for similar experiences that align with God's greater plan. These moments serve as the early stages of a deeper calling and personal participation in the Kingdom's advancement.

During his time as God's chosen leader for the Hebrew Israelite people, Moses experienced multiple divine visions that shaped his leadership. These included a vision of God Himself, the revelation of the Ten Commandments, a vision of a celestial figure, and a vision of God's future plans. Each of these moments defined and cultivated Moses's leadership and legacy.

As mentioned earlier, Moses' young contemporary, Joshua, was blessed to spend forty years under his mentorship. Through this long period, Joshua had the opportunity to observe firsthand how Moses responded to the visions God gave him. He saw how those divine interactions shaped Moses's decisions and guided the people toward the fulfillment of God's promises. Joshua's mentorship under Moses was not just about learning practical leadership; it was a spiritual preparation—an apprenticeship in being led by God.

When Moses' time as leader came to an end, God appointed Joshua to take his place and lead the Israelites into Canaan. Joshua was now tasked with guiding the people through military campaigns, beginning with the pivotal battle of Jericho. In preparation for that moment, Joshua experienced a profound vision:

"He looked up and saw a man standing in front of him with a drawn sword in his hand. Joshua went up to him and asked, 'Are you for us or for our enemies?' 'Neither,' he replied, 'but as commander of the army of the Lord I have now come.' Then Joshua fell facedown to the ground in reverence and asked him, 'What message does my Lord have for his servant?' The commander of the Lord's army replied, 'Take off your sandals, for the place where you are standing is holy.' And Joshua did so." (Joshua 5:13–15, NIV)

This vision confirmed that Joshua was now being led directly by God. Just as Moses had encountered God at the burning bush and was told to remove his sandals, so too was Joshua called onto sacred ground - to be engulfed with God's divine presence, to be defined by His purpose. His leadership was no longer just shaped by Moses' influence; it was now marked by his own encounters with God.

Christian leaders serve as powerful examples to their followers, allowing them to not only witness what God has revealed but also to respond in faith. Through this modeling, followers are prepared for their own future roles as leaders. Within the visions God gives to develop current leaders, He often includes glimpses of the next generation. Such mentors are given insight into those whom God is raising to lead in the future.

We see this clearly in the life of the prophet Samuel, who was given a vision of both Saul and David. Though vastly different, each would shape the destiny of God's people in profound ways. As leaders, God not only gives us a view of our own future in His hands—He also reveals the future He is crafting in the hands of those who follow us.

Once God makes the picture clear and gives the directive, our responsibility becomes twofold: to walk faithfully in our calling and to prepare those whom God has identified to lead next. By doing so, we ensure that the impact of God's Kingdom continues beyond our leadership, carried forward by those who have been shown the way by God through the leaders next to them. In essence, our visions as leaders inspire the visions of the leaders to come, motivating them in their future roles to be effective.

SEVEN QUESTIONS TO ADVANCE THE UNDERSTANDING OF VISION FOR CHRISTIAN LEADERSHIP SUCCESS

1. In your opinion, what is a God-given vision?
2. Do you believe that all authentic Christian leaders receive visions from God? Please explain why or why not.
3. Have you ever experienced a vision from God as a Christian Leader? If so, please describe.
4. As a Christian leader, how does your Biblical comprehension aid in understanding the meaning of your God-given visions?
5. How would you decipher the difference between your aspirations and goals against a God-given vision regarding your Christian leadership objectives?
6. As a Christian leader, how would you respond to a colleague's stated God-given vision that does not align with recognized Christian values and Biblical standards?
7. Once you respond to a vision God gives, in what ways would you measure its fulfillment as a success for the Body of Christ?

CHAPTER SIX
(KEY FIVE): WISDOM

Back in eighth grade, if you had asked me who I admired most, my answer would have been surprising: one of my classmates. His name was Roy, and to me, Roy had it all. He dressed in the latest styles, spoke fluently in the trendiest slang, had strong grades, was well-liked by the school's administration, could dance and rap effortlessly, and—yes—the girls adored him. As far as I was concerned back then, Roy was the man.

While I admired him for all those things (especially the attention from the girls), what truly formed a bond between us went deeper. There was something intangible about Roy—something that set him apart and made me look at him differently than I did the rest of my classmates.

Then one day, something happened that caught all of our attention. One of our classmates arrived at school not by using the normal bus, but by himself, he drove a car to school. For eighth graders, that alone was enough to spark awe. But it wasn't just that he drove—it was what he drove. The car Jerry pulled up in was what many of us would've called a *dream car*.

It was spotless, the tires gleamed with chrome rims, and everything about it was designed to impress. And impress it did. He circled the school five times, making sure we all noticed. His windows were down, and he was blasting the most popular songs of the time. Doing this garnered him much attention, as he drove back and forth passed the school. All of this was calculated by him to project himself in a way that surpassed the coolness we lacked. Of course, it worked. And it wasn't just the girls flocking around Jerry when he finally parked and strolled into the building- we, his friends, gathered around him too, offering our admiration and hyping him up as he walked in. Someone asked, "Whose car is that?" Jerry, with a grin, responded, "Mine." He added, "I was late because I just went and picked it up. You like it?"

I was among those nodding and thinking to myself, *That car is sweet*. Honestly, all of us were enamored. The energy in the room shifted, especially when Jerry offered to take a few of us for a ride after school to grab pizza. Everyone was thrilled—everyone *except* Roy.

Roy didn't seem impressed. He didn't react like the rest of us. Instead, he appeared distant—hesitant even. While we were buzzing with excitement, Roy stood still, his body language unreadable. He didn't respond to Jerry's invitation with the same enthusiasm we did, and it made me pause, if only for a second.

When the final bell that closed the school day rang, anticipation boiled over. We all rushed outside, eager for the post-school joyride. We waited near the courtyard, scanning the corner for Jerry's car to appear. And when he finally pulled up beside the school buses, music blaring, looking every bit like a scene out of a music video, all eyes were on him.

He waved us over, and we started walking toward the car—everyone except Roy. I was just about to follow the group when I heard Roy softly mumble, "I don't think so.

Something's not right with this." His words made me pause. I turned and asked, "Why do you think so?"

Roy said, "Something's not right with this. It doesn't add up. The brother is our age, meaning he has no license. Without a license, how could he buy a car? And not just any car—that car, which runs close to fifty grand. No, something's wrong with this, and I can't get close to it. This doesn't seem like it's going to end well."

I heard Roy—but I also saw that car. And boy, oh boy, it looked like a dream. All our friends were surrounding it, hyped, asking for a ride. Jerry, grinning widely, made sure the last seat was saved just for me.

I took two more steps toward the car, but something Roy said echoed inside me. *It doesn't add up.* He wasn't wrong. Without knowing all the details, what we *did* know didn't make sense. As much as I wanted to join in, a question surfaced in my mind, louder than the music pouring out of Jerry's speakers: *Is this right?*

I didn't get in the car that day. I couldn't fully explain why at the time, but something held me back. Roy, on the other hand, knew exactly what was off. And what he said reminded me of something my mother used to tell me often:

"One day, you, Arthor, will have to make decisions. Some will seem small, others large. But whether small or large, you'll be responsible for them. So, make good ones—ones you won't struggle to live with."

I'd heard her say that many times, but I didn't fully grasp the weight of her words until the next day.

The next day at school, our friend Aimee came up to Roy and me with the classic opener: "Did you hear?"

She didn't wait for a response.

She told us how, later that same day, Jerry and the friends who'd gotten in the car with him were driving along one of the town's back roads when a state police cruiser pulled behind them, lights flashing. Instead of pulling over, Jerry hit the gas. What followed was a high-speed chase—on a winding, uneven road filled with sharp curves, sudden stops, and unpredictable traffic.

At one point, Jerry was clocked going eighty-five miles per hour—in a thirty-mile-per-hour zone.

Eventually, he lost control. The car slammed into a telephone pole. The force of the crash ejected Jerry and two others from the vehicle. None of them had been wearing seat belts. The other passengers, still inside the car, were also seriously injured. They were all rushed to the hospital by ambulance. But the aftermath didn't end there.

When the police searched the wrecked car, they found felony-level drugs, two small containers of alcohol, and discovered that the car was stolen. That was why the chase began in the first place. Jerry and our friends, now bruised and broken, had a much bigger problem on their hands than we could've ever imagined.

Thank God no one died that day, but everyone involved was severely injured. And because of the drugs, the alcohol, and the fact that the car was stolen, they all faced felony charges. The weight of it all settled in slowly, and as I processed what had happened, I looked at Roy and asked, "How did you know?"

He replied simply, "I didn't, but it didn't add up. My grandfather always said, 'If it doesn't add up, it doesn't make sense. And if it doesn't make sense, don't touch it.'"

Roy paused for a moment before continuing, "God has given everyone the ability to judge, analyze, and understand things in a way that helps us avoid situations that would harm us—physically, emotionally, or spiritually. The real problem we all face is using that ability effectively and then trusting what our instincts, or better yet, God's guidance, are telling us."

He looked me in the eye, his expression serious, and said, "By doing this, we avoid regret. More importantly, we keep ourselves out of trouble—out of the hospital, and out of jail, like those guys."

With a half-smile, he added, "Art, be wise in your ways. Use what God gave Solomon, my brother." What he was really saying was, "Use common sense. Use the wisdom that's in that big head of yours."

I would never have known if my life had been saved that day by listening to Roy, but I saw the consequences that came when my friends did not listen and adhere to the wisdom that God had given Roy that day. Because they refused to listen, they were forced to face severe consequences. Because of this, most of my friends involved, once they recovered, did not return to school because they were sent to a youth detention center or an academy for troubled teens.

What I learned for sure was that the use of wisdom is important and it should be taken seriously because if I hadn't, the consequences would have been indeed serious. I learned that day that both Roy and my mom were right. The ability to judge wisely and make decisions based on God's guidance wasn't just important—it was life-saving.

At age thirteen, my friend Roy introduced me to wisdom in a way I had never experienced before. Roy didn't have all the answers about the car—how Jerry acquired it or where it was headed—but he understood that aligning himself with Jerry in that moment would put everything he stood for at risk. Roy wasn't just avoiding a dangerous situation, he was protecting his integrity, his identity, and the future he knew God had planned for him. He told me that wisdom was the guiding force that led him to hold onto his values. He didn't allow himself to be swayed by the allure of a shiny object or the excitement of being part of something that seemed impressive but ultimately dangerous. Wisdom, Roy explained, was about seeing beyond the surface and understanding the long-term impact of every decision. It was about making choices that wouldn't just benefit you in the moment, but that would align with who you were and who you were becoming. From that point, something shifted in me. I realized that wisdom wasn't just a thing to be admired from afar—it was something to be sought after, something to be learned and applied in my own life. I made a decision right then and there to go on a mission to become more knowledgeable about wisdom. I wanted to understand how to use it to guide my own decisions, to help me see beyond temptations and distractions, and to build a life that would reflect my integrity, my purpose, and ultimately, my faith. Wisdom Defined.

In Christian leadership, wisdom begins with an understanding of who God is—His nature, His sovereignty, and His ways. Psalm 111:10 highlights that the fear of the Lord is the starting point of wisdom. This reverence for God isn't about being afraid of Him in a conventional sense, but about acknowledging His authority and recognizing His holiness and majesty. The fear of the Lord is the first step in a leader's spiritual formation. It is the attitude of humility that allows a leader to submit to God's guidance, to listen to His word, and to obey His commands, trusting that God's way is always the best way.

As William McDonald points out, obedience to God is a critical part of this process. Spiritual knowledge and wisdom are unlocked through obedience. The more a leader submits to God's will and follows His precepts, the more they receive divine understanding and insight. Wisdom, then, is not merely intellectual knowledge; it is a living, active response to God's **word** that shapes decisions, actions, and relationships. This is why the Christian leader's ability to lead with wisdom is closely tied to their ability to obey and trust in God's plan.

John MacArthur further underscores that wisdom, as it pertains to leadership, begins with a redemptive relationship with God. A leader can have knowledge or intellectual capacity, but true wisdom comes only through a relationship with God that is rooted in reverential awe. This relationship is foundational to understanding truth and to navigating life's complexities in a way that honors God. Without this relationship, a leader is unable to possess the ultimate wisdom necessary for effective leadership.

The key difference between worldly wisdom and Godly wisdom is this: Worldly wisdom often relies on human understanding and reasoning, while Godly wisdom starts with a reverence for God's will and a submission to His authority. It's through this lens that a Christian leader must approach every decision, every challenge, and every relationship. God's word, through the Holy Spirit, is the guiding force that enables Christian leaders to make wise decisions that align with His will.

In defining wisdom, it is important to recognize that wisdom is not merely about making wise decisions. It encompasses discerning God's will and leading with a heart surrendered to Him (Blackaby, 2020). Wisdom also goes beyond intellectual knowledge; it involves applying life experiences and spiritual understanding to decision making. It reflects a leader's maturity, the ability to learn from both success and failure, and the capacity to see God's hand at work in all circumstances (BCM, 2023).

Vines connects wisdom to the Hebrew term *chakam*, which means wise or to act wisely. From a religious perspective, *chakam* points to wisdom originating from the understanding that God is the source of all wisdom. It is through the willing acceptance of the fear of God—living in accordance with His expectations—that one demonstrates true wisdom. Additionally, the term *chokmah* is linked to wisdom, meaning the knowledge and ability to make the right choices at the right time. It is the consistency of making correct decisions that signifies a mature, wise individual. Wisdom, then, is the yearning and desire for the fear of the Lord. For leaders, it is an understanding that, with all their being, they are walking ... striving to follow Jesus Christ and the example he set (Strongs, 1798).

Seen as more of a problem-solving skill, Northouse defines wisdom as the ability to evaluate the appropriateness of alternative approaches within the specific context or setting in which a leader acts (Northouse, 2022). For leaders, wisdom enables them to make sound judgments and decisions. It encourages leaders to seek what is right and true based on God's will, rather than on personal feelings or thoughts.

Furthermore, wisdom is the recognition of the faith and abilities leaders have been entrusted with, and it involves applying these gifts with the responsibility to follow through with diligence and vigor. Wisdom provides leaders with the temperament, balance, and perspective they need to influence and help others without imposing their personal inclinations (such as being condescending). Leaders, while guiding others, are to grow in the wisdom of the Lord, understand their own capacities, and recognize where opportunities exist so they can navigate and grow effectively— ultimately carrying out their work to glorify the Lord (Krejcir, 2022).

Clearly, this highlights how wisdom is connected with vision (an earlier discussed key) for the Christian leader.

For the purposes of this writing, wisdom will also be viewed as a "key"—understood as knowledge and experience that can be shared for the benefit of others. Additionally, wisdom is truth applied in specific situations for Godly purposes. The wisdom that God provides to leaders helps them see situations, circumstances, problems, and opportunities from a Godly perspective, through a biblical lens.

Christian leaders eagerly desire to share insights that will help others live better lives by doing what God desires, while also exhorting truth about how followers should avoid the things that the Lord disapproves of. Since Godly wisdom is essential for being an effective leader—one who exemplifies

God's ways—wisdom becomes both a constant attribute and an indispensable tool for leaders, guiding them through the many challenges they face (Kelleher, 2023).

For effective leadership, wisdom is not only essential but also a necessary key, as leaders will use it to guide people toward a way of life that aligns with both the created order and God's redemptive work. In the Old Testament, wisdom is rooted in the fear of the Lord; in the New Testament, wisdom is further amplified and reoriented around Christ (Ebert, 2025).

THE APOSTLE PAUL

For Christian leaders, it is not enough to simply acquire or possess wisdom; the crucial factor is how and when they use the leadership "key" when it is needed most. A prime example of this is Solomon, particularly in the story where he had to discern which of the two women was the true birth mother of the child who survived what seemed to be an unfortunate accident. After one woman switched her deceased child with the living one, the real mother woke to find her child had died. Solomon resolved the confusion by exercising his wisdom. After determining the truth, those who witnessed the judgment recognized that such a superior level of discernment must have been a gift from the heavenly Father (1 Kings 3:16-28, NIV).

Throughout Scripture, God demonstrates the many ways wisdom should be used as a leadership "key." A notable example is found in the events surrounding the apostle Paul, who was placed on a ship bound for Italy after appealing to Caesar regarding charges against him. Following a spiritually endorsed fast, Paul discerned that continuing the voyage would lead to disaster. Not only would they lose the cargo and the ship, but they would also risk losing lives. Empowered by the Holy Spirit, Paul warned them that the journey should not proceed. Despite their failure, he assured them that, although the ship would be destroyed, no lives would be lost (Acts 27:9-12, NIV).

Soon after, unfortunately, Paul's foresight concerning what was to come became their reality. The ship encountered storms and extreme difficulties, forcing the crew to abandon much of their cargo and take drastic measures to prevent the ship from capsizing and, even worse, being destroyed. As the nightmare of their journey continued, they also spent days traveling in complete darkness, which led them to believe they would not survive and that doom was inevitable.

In the midst of this, Paul, having fasted once more, reminded the ship's leaders of his earlier warning not to sail at that particular time. However, he assured them that, although the ship would be destroyed, no lives would be lost.

Paul, though in chains, did what Christian leaders are called to do: he turned to God in times of peril. Paul remained open to God's guidance, and an angel appeared to him, reassuring him not to fear. The angel made it clear that Paul's mission was not over— he was destined to stand before Caesar. Later, as the ship drew near land, Paul, confident in God's promises, urged everyone on board to eat, knowing that their strength would be needed.

As God had told Paul, the ship began to break apart, forcing everyone aboard to jump into the sea, swimming and clinging to pieces of the wreckage. They made their way to an island called Malta, where they were all saved, just as the Lord had promised— none perished.

Paul, like Solomon, exemplifies a crucial aspect of wisdom. However, true wisdom cannot exist without God's guidance. In reality, wisdom is the willingness—and the ability—to heed God's direction, both when we seek Him in times of need and when He offers His instruction to Christian leaders. Without God, individuals are left to rely on their own understanding, which may provide short-term solutions. These short-term solutions often miss out on the long-term purposes that God has established, which may surpass our ability to comprehend.

Take Paul's situation as an example. He was in chains, a prisoner under duress, and his circumstances seemed beyond his control. While this was the visible reality, Paul recognized that something spiritual was unfolding—that there was a greater purpose behind his situation. This understanding is born from God-given wisdom. This leads leaders to seek God in a way that allows their decisions to strengthen and inspire their faith, as well as inspire and strengthen the faith of those following their lead.

If Paul had relied solely on his own abilities, both he and the others aboard the ship would have perished. But Paul did not lead based on his own wisdom. Instead, he sought the Lord, who provided the direction and discernment he needed. This divine guidance not only preserved their lives but also planted seeds of faith in the hearts of those aboard (Acts 27:21-38, NIV).

This is wisdom. It is a gift from God, given to leaders, but it is used through His direction to lead others according to God's will—not their own. The familiar scripture reminds us all, especially leaders, to "trust in the LORD with all your heart and lean not on your own understanding; in all your ways submit to him, and he will make your paths straight" (Proverbs 3:5-6, NIV). The willingness to hear, listen, and obey God's guidance is the key to effective leadership. What distinguishes a leader of the world from one ordained by Christ is their response to this calling. Effectively utilizing this wisdom is the key to true leadership.

WHY WISDOM IS IMPORTANT TO CHRISTIAN LEADERSHIP

Leaders, particularly within the Christian faith, are sacred and essential. They are called to carry out many responsibilities and to be present in the lives of those God has ordained to surround them. God positions Christian leaders to assist in decision-making, problem-solving, and critical thinking. They are tasked with managing, untangling, and reshaping the lives of Christ's followers, as well as making decisions regarding resources (which will be discussed in the next chapter), all while navigating both times of ease and moments of pressure when information and assistance may be limited (BCM, 2023).

Within the context of a Christian institution, there have been—and will continue to be—moments when the correct application of wisdom is imperative, not only for the leader but also for those impacted by the leader's decisions and actions.

So, why is wisdom important? The Holy Spirit, through Solomon, offers an explanation:

"My son, do not let wisdom and understanding out of your sight, preserve sound judgment and discretion; they will be life for you, an ornament to grace your neck. Then you will go on your way in safety, and your foot will not stumble." (Proverbs 3:21-23, NIV)

Solomon emphasizes that wisdom (which brings a sense of understanding) should always remain close, never out of sight. Wisdom is a vital attribute and tool for all phases of life and leadership, often guiding leaders in preserving sound judgment and exercising discretion. Wisdom should be constantly worn, meaning it should be evident in the leader's actions and decisions. Whether in decision-making or in discerning whether something is of God or not (discernment), wisdom is key.

Wisdom is not self-attained, although the world we live in often believes this to be true. Even if we were to say that wisdom comes through experience, it still points to wisdom being God-given, as the very experiences we encounter are ordained by God. Wisdom comes from God, and He gives it with a purpose. Wisdom is the foundation for discernment, which is an essential tool for Christian leaders.

Discerning what to say, what not to say, how to say it, when to say it, and to whom to say it—all of this is rooted in wisdom. Wisdom enables leaders to perceive the truth beyond the words spoken by others and to clarify the meaning behind uncertain situations. However, when dissolved is desired or needed, it is important to remember that wisdom is a gift that Christians must seek and receive from God. Too often, we attempt to rely on our own wisdom, which might work occasionally, but more often than not, it leads to dilemmas that, in our own strength, we cannot resolve.

Wisdom helps us make sound decisions, but it can only do so when we turn to God. This is where both spiritual and personal growth occur. But such wisdom is only available when God speaks and directs. It is in this obedience to God's guidance that wisdom is displayed. A leader experiences wisdom when they follow the directives God gives and acknowledge His guidance in all decisions (Krejcir, 2002).

The statement many individuals often make after creating a mess of a situation is: "How did I get into this, and how do I get out?" In a sense, this is a prayer to God (though it could be more eloquently worded). Either way, we are asking God for His voice and His intervention in our situation. The challenge, however, is that self-reliant wisdom often leads us to disregard God's direction, leading us as leaders to fail to seek Him at all, both of which are rooted in pride and self-righteousness.

For leaders, wisdom is a collaborative effort between themselves and God to accomplish what God has called them to do. As leaders, we turn to God to ensure we are heading in the right direction, handling our responsibilities according to His commands, and avoiding shortsightedness (lack of vision). Wisdom helps us not only move forward ourselves but also lead others toward the goal God has established.

Wisdom is a confession that, as leaders, we cannot do it alone. We are wise enough to acknowledge that without God, we are doomed. However, with Him, the visions for success He has placed in our hearts for His church and kingdom purposes will not fail. Instead, they will prevail, developing into what He has called forth (Magnelli, 2020).

John Piper writes: *"The reason I say that the greatest human wisdom has the greatest likelihood of success in achieving the intended, righteous goal is that only God never fails in the achievement of His intended goals. The wisdom of God, His general knowledge of reality, His situational insight, and His necessary resolve always succeed in achieving His intended goals."* (2024)

So why is wisdom important for the Christian leader? The key question is not "if" but "when" your role as a leader will be tested—and it will be tested in various ways. Wisdom is what you use to pass the test successfully and overcome the challenges. Again, wisdom is about using what God has given us as leaders so that His glory is revealed. However, we must turn to Him in those moments of need and seek the wisdom He offers. James tells us, *"If any of you lacks wisdom, you should ask God, who gives generously to all without finding fault, and it will be given to you"* (James 1:5, NIV).

God will complement the wisdom He has already gifted us as leaders with additional insight to meet the challenges ahead. However, the crucial element that brings forth great wisdom is God Himself. As His leaders, we must turn to Him—not only to hear His voice but to act in full obedience to what He tells us.

WISDOM APPLIED

Pastor Jim Cymbala exemplified wisdom during his early trials at the Brooklyn Tabernacle. In the early years of his church in the struggling area of Brooklyn, New York, the church was rundown—both the meeting place and the congregation were in disarray. With fewer than two dozen parishioners and a pile of bills, Pastor Cymbala and his wife, Carol, felt lost and unsure of how to overcome their difficulties.

After accepting an invitation for a prayer retreat in Florida, Pastor Cymbala cried out to God, seeking guidance and direction. During the retreat, God spoke to him, giving clear instructions on how to move forward: "Lead my people to pray and call upon My name." God promised that if they prioritized prayer, they would lack nothing. God would provide a word to preach and financial support for both the church and his family. Even more, God assured Pastor Cymbala that they would never have a building in Brooklyn large enough to contain the crowds that would come as a result of their faithfulness.

Pastor Cymbala heard from God, which is always significant. More importantly, he responded by dedicating his entire ministry to following God's directive (Cymbala, 2018). To this very day, as I visit Brooklyn and witness all that God has done for and through that ministry, it is clear that they embraced God's call. Pastor Cymbala, who takes no credit for the success achieved on Smith Street in Brooklyn today, is widely regarded as a sagacious leader. Why? Because he called out to God, God responded, and he faithfully followed the directive given to him.

As leaders, like Pastor Cymbala, we will encounter challenges in many forms. But when we call out to God and follow His guidance, He will provide us with His wisdom, ensuring that His will is done.

"For the Lord gives wisdom; from His mouth come knowledge and understanding" (Prov. 2:6, NIV). Wisdom is

not just a key for successful leadership; as we see, it is essential for effective Christian leadership. However, we must remember that the source— and the only true source— of wisdom is God. For leaders to be effective, wisdom is necessary. Yet, leaders will only receive or recognize this wisdom through direct dialogue with God (prayer) and obedience to His directive on how it should be applied.

It is in our obedient response to God's charge where wisdom is visible. And, properly handling what God deems as correct leads toward effective Christian leadership.

Seven Questions to Advance the Understanding of Wisdom for Christian Leadership Success

1. How would you define wisdom?

2. How important do you believe the correct understanding and use of wisdom is to the Christian leader?

3. Who was a leader that you believed excelled in wisdom? In what ways did you see them utilize the wisdom they possessed?

4. Where has the use of wisdom been instrumental in your leadership approach and response?

5. In your opinion, in what ways does humility impart wisdom?

6. Do you believe age impacts the proper utilization of wisdom? Please explain how it does or does not.

7. Do you believe cultural traditions impact the proper utilization of wisdom? Please explain how it does or does not.

CHAPTER SEVEN
(KEY SIX)
STEWARDSHIP

For some reason, my marriage is often a topic of conversation. Maybe it's because when people look at me and then at my wife, they wonder, "How did she fall for him?" She is undeniably beautiful—my gift from God—and to this day, I can't fully explain how I was blessed with her.

There's a story I like to share when people ask how she came to be fond of me. Back when we were dating, many moons ago, she offered to do something that immediately opened my heart to her: she offered to cook for me. I quickly realized just how smart she was. She clearly understood how to win a man's heart.

In return for her kind offer, I offered to take her to the grocery store. About thirty minutes into our trip, two interesting things happened. First, I noticed she had piled an enormous number of groceries into the cart. I found it curious, since the plan was for her to make just one meal for me. Still, I decided to be patient and see where it would lead.

We arrived at the checkout counter, and I watched as the cart— filled to capacity—was unloaded onto the conveyor belt. The total began to climb: first fifty dollars, then a hundred. Soon, it surpassed two hundred, finally stopping around two hundred and sixty dollars. I couldn't help but wonder: *Does she think I'm some kind of monster who eats this much food?*

But my curiosity was quickly resolved when my soon-to-be wife reached into her pouch and pulled out something I had never used in my life—coupons. Like an angel, before my very eyes, as if she were a financial specialist, she handed the cashier a neat stack of these coupons, and just as I watched and just as I saw the total rise, I now saw it fall. The final amount dropped to about fifty-five dollars.

Amazed, I handed over my credit card, bagged the groceries, and walked briskly out the door, glancing over my shoulder as if I had just committed a robbery.

As we made our way to the car, laughing at my reaction, I— like a gentleman should—helped her into the passenger seat before unloading the groceries into the trunk. Then, according to her account of our experience, I did something she had never seen anyone do before.

After I finished loading up the groceries, I walked across the snowy, frozen parking lot (which I forgot to mention earlier) to return the shopping cart. When I got back and sat in the driver's seat, she stared at me. I asked what was wrong, and she said, "There are people who get paid to do that—to return the carts after we use them."

I replied, "I know, but I believe that if someone allows us to use something for our benefit, we should treat it with respect. Why not make their job easier by returning what we've borrowed? Imagine if there were no carts to use because people abused the privilege."

She thought about it for a moment and told me that my perspective—preserving what belongs to others—was interesting, even amazing. That impression, along with how I handled other things like finances and how she saw me care for others' belongings, helped her decide that I was worthy of her trust. Not long after, she agreed to marry me.

Over time, we've come to see that how we handle the privileges and gifts placed in our hands truly matters. Even now, years later, we still live by those values—something we've come to understand as *stewardship*.

STEWARDSHIP DEFINED

Stewardship is a frequently used term in the modern Christian church. We often hear it mentioned in the context of giving, particularly during the offering portion of a service. Week after week, pastors commission congregants to give by referencing Paul's second letter to the church in Corinth: *"Each of you should give what you have decided in your heart to give, not reluctantly or under compulsion, for God loves a cheerful giver"* (2 Cor. 9:7, NIV).

While giving is certainly a form of stewardship, the concept is not limited to tithes or offerings. True stewardship encompasses far more—it should define the actions, principles, and mindset of every Christian leader.

The word *stewardship* is rooted in the term *steward*, which translates from the Hebrew word *bayith*, and the Greek words *epitropos* and *oikonomos*. All carry the connotation of one who oversees a household or acts as an administrator. A steward, then, is a trustworthy individual entrusted with the responsibility of managing another's possessions (Kamer, 2018).

A more enriched definition describes a steward as one whom the head of a household or property owner entrusts with managing affairs, overseeing finances, and distributing portions appropriately to those in their care (Watson, 2024).

Stewardship for the Christian includes all the previously mentioned aspects, but it also rests on a foundational understanding that deepens its meaning. A Christian steward is called to manage everything God has entrusted to them— faithfully and responsibly— according to biblical principles. This responsibility encompasses a wide range of areas: resources, talents, time, and more. All of these are to be used in ways that ultimately glorify God through service to others.

At its core, stewardship is about recognizing God as the ultimate owner and source of all things. It involves treating every possession and ability as a gift—meant to be used wisely, generously, and with intention. Biblical stewardship teaches that management is not merely about conservation or careful planning, but about active participation in God's purposes for the world and for each believer's life (Ministry Brands, 2024).

The God-given duty of stewardship is first introduced in Scripture at the time of creation, when God says:

> *"Let us make mankind in our image, in our likeness, so that they may rule over the fish in the sea and the birds in the sky, over the livestock and all the wild animals, and over all the creatures that move along the ground."* (Gen. 1:26, NIV)

After issuing this mandate, God created a garden— Eden— where Adam and Eve's stewardship was to begin. Their directive was "to work it and keep it" (Gen. 2:15, NIV), a stewardship charge extended to all human beings, and particularly to believers. Proper stewardship begins with recognizing to whom everything truly belongs. Adam and Eve did not own the garden; they were entrusted with its care.

This understanding remains central for believers today. First, stewardship begins by acknowledging that all we manage ultimately belongs to God. Second, it requires us to handle the responsibilities given to us in a way that aligns with how God would have them done. Stewardship involves exercising God-given dominion over His creation in a way that reflects the image and character of the Creator. For faithful stewards, this means taking seriously the responsibility to maintain, protect, and even beautify what belongs to God (Sproul, 2023). The steward's mindset must always return to this truth: God owns everything, and humanity has been granted dominion not for possession, but for trust and care (Kamer, 2018).

This brings us to the unique meaning of stewardship for the Christian leader. While stewardship applies broadly, the role of a leader carries increased expectations. Unlike secular stewardship, Christian leadership acknowledges God as the ultimate owner and source. The Christian leader is a steward of all that God has entrusted to their care.

Northouse (2022) emphasizes that stewardship in leadership involves taking full responsibility for the role one is given. Leaders are accountable for wisely managing the people and organizations placed under their care—not for personal gain, but for the advancement of God's Kingdom and the betterment of the surrounding society. This responsibility also includes the spiritual well-being of those God has positioned under their leadership. Christian leaders lead with a clear understanding that all they oversee is temporary and ultimately not their own. Their calling is to build upon and enhance each person's contribution toward holistic and spiritually grounded leadership (Rodin, 2010).

Lastly, and most significantly, Christian leaders who understand stewardship recognize that the people they lead belong to God. The individuals they work with, preach to, guide, support, and inspire are God's people, not theirs. One of the most common mistakes that leads to leadership failure is the misbelief that the people are their own to possess and control.

Returning to the creation narrative, God gave Adam and Eve everything—not to own, but to manage responsibly, as He would. Similarly, Christian leaders are entrusted by God with His people, and their role is to reflect God's identity in all they do. We are called to lead in a way that mirrors God's heart, always responding to those in our care with humility, grace, and wisdom.

As faithful stewards, Christian leaders have a distinct responsibility in the way they lead. Through stewardship, they empower their people, delegate authority, value and involve others, and seek the best in and from those they lead. They constantly uplift, encourage, and celebrate those under their care, pushing them into the limelight and rewarding their growth. In doing so, Christian leaders seek to accomplish God's will in the best possible way.

These leaders do not seek self-glorification. Instead, they find their reward in witnessing the growth and development of those called to follow them (Rodin, 2010).

JOSEPH

Joseph's life story is widely recognized, often shared in Sunday schools and church services around the world. As the son of Jacob— who seemed to favor him above all his other children— expectations for a prosperous future were high. His father's favor made Joseph's future seem certain. But everything changed when jealousy overtook his brothers, leading them to sell him into slavery. This act stripped Joseph of the comfort and security he once knew, thrusting him into an unknown world with unfamiliar cultural norms and practices.

In a situation like this, many would have forfeited their integrity, perhaps abandoning their God given identity to fit into the new cultural norm. But Joseph, even in the face of hardship, held on to who he was. He never compromised the identity bestowed upon him by his earthly father or his heavenly Father.

After being sold, Joseph was taken to Egypt by the Midianites. There, he was eventually placed in the service of one of Pharaoh's top officials, Potiphar, the captain of the guard. Potiphar was powerful, wealthy, and perceptive—so perceptive that he recognized something special in Joseph. He could sense that the Lord was with him. As a result, Potiphar made Joseph his personal attendant and put him in charge of his entire household. From that point on, everything Potiphar owned was entrusted to Joseph's care. And because God was with Joseph, Potiphar's household— and all that he owned, both in the house and in the field— was richly blessed (Gen. 39:1-6, NIV).

Despite his excellent handling of Potiphar's affairs, the dynamic between them shifted after an illicit incident. Potiphar's wife asked Joseph to sleep with her, but when he refused, she falsely accused him of attempted rape. Upon hearing the charges, Potiphar removed Joseph, from his position as a trusted servant, was sent to prison.

In this moment, we see several key principles in action. First is integrity. Joseph refused to allow the temptation from Potiphar's wife to compromise the man God had called him to be. A wrongful affair would not only tarnish his character before his master but also before God. Next is wisdom. It was God's wisdom in Joseph that enabled him to bring success to Potiphar's household, and it would sustain him through these trying times. Joseph's leadership—his ability to manage resources and navigate crises—demonstrates the critical role of wisdom in effective stewardship. His stewardship approach was rooted in honoring God and serving others, underscoring the importance of leadership driven by stewardship principles (Baker, 2023).

Finally, Joseph's faith held him strong, even after being betrayed by his brothers and uncertain about his future. Rather than being weakened by his circumstances, he drew strength from his belief that God had a purpose for his life, even in the midst of trial. This unwavering faith laid the foundation for his ability to steward his life effectively.

After a stint in prison, Joseph was released at Pharaoh's request to interpret a troubling dream. Due to his accurate interpretation, along with the other qualities of his character (mentioned earlier), Pharaoh appointed Joseph as governor over all of Egypt. His responsibilities included overseeing the allocation of food supplies during the seven years of surplus, as well as managing resources during the subsequent seven years of famine, which Joseph had predicted through Pharaoh's dream.

Several important lessons emerge from these events. First, despite the hostile and complex circumstances surrounding him, Joseph recognized that everything taking place, though it involved him, was not ultimately about him. He never victimized himself. This reflects the mindset of a true steward— someone who understands their role and appropriately handles the situation before them knowing it is a part of God's larger plan.

Second, Joseph recognized that his role in managing Potiphar's and Pharaoh's affairs was an opportunity to exercise stewardship. He understood that the resources he handled, whether time, money, or goods, belonged to someone else—not him. His responsibility was to allocate these resources according to the needs and demands of his masters. Joseph's wise management led to success for both Potiphar and Pharaoh, and ultimately, to his own advancement.

Finally, as a steward, Joseph embraced a larger vision—his actions and self-denial impacted not only those around him but also his own family. His brothers, who once betrayed him, would one day come to him seeking food during the famine. Joseph's stewardship had a ripple effect, saving the lives of many, including those who had wronged him. Trusting that the Lord was with him, Joseph stewarded the gifts, opportunities, and resources God had entrusted to him with excellence and faithfulness. His stewardship played a vital part in God's plan to save Israel and Egypt from starvation (Turner, 2021).

Christian leaders should draw inspiration from Joseph's trials and victories, as they are called to care for God's people and their needs, just as Joseph was entrusted with the care of Potiphar's household and Pharaoh's kingdom. Like Joseph, we are not the owners of the resources entrusted to us. We are stewards, caretakers of all that God places in our hands during our time as Kingdom leaders, with the ultimate goal of serving Him effectively.

WHY STEWARDSHIP IS IMPORTANT TO THE CHRISTIAN LEADER

Stewardship should be critical to the Christian leader because it reflects the understanding that everything we have been entrusted with is not our own, but belongs to God. Scripture clearly reminds us, "The earth is the Lord's, and everything in it, the world, and all who live in it" (Psalm 24:1, NIV).

If we reflect once again on Joseph, it was his faithfulness in stewardship that preserved the nation of Israel. His wise and faithful handling of resources ultimately paved the way for the Messiah and our salvation. In the same way, our stewardship as Christian leaders—over all of God's resources, particularly the people He has called us to shepherd—has a far-reaching impact. If we handle these responsibilities with integrity and faithfulness, it will contribute to the furtherance of His kingdom and purpose on earth.

Our position and duty as stewarding Christian leaders are clearly illustrated by a parable Jesus shared about being prepared for His return:

"For it will be like a man going on a journey, who called his servants and entrusted to them his property. To one he gave five talents, to another two, to another one, each according to his ability. Then he went away. The servant who had received the five talents went at once and traded with them, and he made five more. Similarly, the one who had received two talents made two more. But the servant who had received one talent went and dug in the ground and hid his master's money." (Matt. 25:14-18, NIV)

This passage underscores the importance of exceptional stewardship for Christian leaders. It begins with the fundamental truth that everything belongs to God. Secondly, as leaders, we must understand that because everything belongs to God, we will be held accountable when the Lord returns. He will seek an updated report on what we have done with what He has entrusted to us. Christ will ask whether we have faithfully pursued the tasks He placed in our hearts for His people, His church, and His world. He will want to know if we have handled everything responsibly.

However, many Christian leaders today, much like in the parable, have chosen to go their own way. By failing to continue their personal transformation, their behavior reflects a disregard for the truth that what they possess belongs to God. Just as in the parable, God will expect a clear account of what we've done with the time, talents, and resources He has provided. We will be required to explain our efforts—or the lack thereof—and be held accountable for both our actions and inactions. Furthermore, the consequences of our disobedience affect those we lead. Our failure to properly handle God's possessions can influence our followers in a negative way, reflecting the same disregard for stewardship that we, as leaders, have unknowingly modeled (Mather, 2024).

Therefore, as leaders, we must remember that we are not only accountable for our own behavior, but also for the impact that our actions have on those who follow us. As influential individuals in God's Kingdom, we must be mindful of the example we set.

Our motive as leaders should not be to avoid ridicule from the Master, as seen in the parable. Instead, our mission must always be aimed at pleasing the Lord. This becomes possible when stewardship is a priority. Not only are we gratified when our duties align with God's expectations, but it is a true blessing to hear from the Lord what the faithful servants in the parable heard: "Well done, my good and faithful servant. You have been faithful over a little; I will set you over much. Enter into the joy of your master" (Matt. 25:23, NIV).

The Apostle Paul refers to ministers as stewards of the mysteries of God (1 Cor. 4:1, NIV), and Peter speaks of all Christians as good stewards of God's varied grace (1 Peter 4:10, NIV). Clearly, stewardship is central to Christian leadership. Leaders who excel in stewardship often possess the ability to influence, handle authority well, and are more trustworthy (Mohler, 2025). Stewardship highlights just how much God entrusts to us, His fallible and frail creatures. As we noted earlier, we are all called to exercise dominion over creation—not as owners, but as caretakers (Frank, 2022).

Moreover, effective stewardship underscores our assignment as leaders: to serve one another at the behest of God.

STEWARDSHIP APPLIED

John Wesley once preached, "When the Possessor of heaven and earth brought you into being and placed you in this world, He placed you here not as a proprietor, but as a steward" (Sproul, 2023). Stewards are managers, and good managers seek to please the ones they serve. Joseph served both Potiphar and later Pharaoh. Yet, even when he had command of nearly everything, he laid his hands on, he still recognized who his true Master was (Turner, 2021).

Christian leaders are most effective when they apply the "key" of stewardship. Stewardship keeps them focused on the ultimate objective that God sets before them: His people. At the same time, it conditions Christian leaders to always remember to whom everything they handle truly belongs. Stewardship serves as a reminder that all things in their hands ultimately belong to God.

For the Christian leader, stewardship becomes a mindset, a motivational and connecting tool that acknowledges God as the ultimate owner of everything we possess. When Stewardship is applied to a leader's approach, both the leader and their followers will benefit.

STEWARDSHIP BENEFITS:

1. Spiritual growth and maturity

The way a Christian leader responds to the stewardship "key" reflects their spiritual maturity. Simply choosing to embrace it leads to greater effectiveness. However, the true power of stewardship lies in its ability to foster spiritual growth. As a leader learns to manage resources in a God-honoring way, guided by His directives, they not only grow and mature spiritually, but their actions also benefit the Kingdom of God and the people they serve.

2. An enriched intimacy with God

Christian leaders, through stewardship, cultivate a deep, intimate relationship with Jesus. By faithfully handling what He entrusts to His chosen leaders, a profound camaraderie develops between master and servant, Savior and sinner, and the true Lord and His children. This is the kind of relationship He desires to have with each of us, rooted in trust.

We grow closer to God when we begin to see ourselves as He sees us and recognizes that He entrusts us, His leaders, with what He holds most sacred: the lives, hearts, and the opportunity to lead others to Him. When a leader grasps this truth, their relationship with God evolves. Often, their life and leadership are transformed, becoming defined by the love that God continually shares with them.

3. A greater confidence in God's voice and His directives

Christian leaders, through stewardship, cultivate a deep and intimate relationship with Jesus. By faithfully managing what He entrusts to His chosen leaders, a profound camaraderie forms between master and servant, Savior and sinner, and the true Lord and His children. This is the relationship He desires to have with each of us, grounded in trust.

We draw closer to God when we begin to see ourselves as He sees us and recognize that He entrusts us, His leaders, with what He holds most sacred: the lives, hearts, and the opportunity to lead others to Him. When a leader fully grasps this truth, their relationship with God evolves. Their life and leadership are often transformed, becoming defined by the love God continually pours into them.

4. Impacts followers, provoking spiritual development.

Stewardship calls for a fundamental shift in how we view leadership—away from a hierarchical model centered on the leader, and toward a practice of leading that is available to everyone (Vanourek, 2022). When Christian leaders openly demonstrate how they steward both God's resources and the people entrusted to their care—how they respond, guide, and, most importantly, love others as God would—they inspire deeper growth in faith, grace, and mercy among their followers.

Through this experience, followers begin to emulate the behaviors they observe in their leaders, ultimately becoming leaders themselves. Whether in the home, the church, the workplace, or their community, the dynamic fostered by stewardship leads to spiritual growth and development for followers, a process that never ends. It continues, fueled by the same love that Jesus shows to those He leads.

Leaders shape their followers through influence, shared values, and principles, just as Christ does. As leaders allow their stewardship to be seen, they inspire followers to become stewards in turn. Over time, these followers develop into the next generation of leaders.

5. Christian Leader Stewardship Results in God's Glorification

God expects all people, especially Christian leaders, to practice stewardship in ways that glorify Him and strengthen His Kingdom on earth. Since everything belongs to God, the things He places in the hands of His leaders offer new opportunities to serve others and share the love of Christ. When leaders follow His guidance in handling these responsibilities, they bring glory to God. His name is made known to those who do not yet know Him, and misconceptions about who Jesus is are corrected.

Stewardship is more than just managing resources; it is an opportunity to love and serve others according to God's will. Through the acts and works of stewardship, leaders reflect God's image, showing the world His character through their service. It is crucial to remember that stewardship, in all its forms, is fundamentally about service. Leaders are called to serve others and to use what God has entrusted to them to guide the lost to Him. Throughout this process, God calls His leaders to steward everything He has given with holiness and righteousness. The ultimate purpose of stewardship is to glorify God. Leaders who seek to honor God in their calling are preparing for the day when others will take up the mantle and continue the mission of Christ's Great Commission.

A Christian leader is a steward entrusted with the responsibility of caring for others and managing valuable resources. It is a position of trust, where one is called to be the guardian of what God has entrusted to them. Building a culture of stewardship requires a fundamental shift in how we understand and practice leadership. It is not merely about being a good leader; stewardship empowers a Christian leader to be truly effective.

Seven Questions to Advance the Understanding of Stewardship for Christian Leadership Success

1. How would you define Biblical stewardship?
2. Besides finances, in what other categories do you find stewardship employed in the Christian faith?
3. Do you implore stewardship practices to shape your personal life? If you are willing, please describe how.
4. In what ways would stewardship influence your leadership approach?
5. How could stewardship, if mismanaged, impact the church, institution, or organization you lead?
6. How do you model stewardship principles into your public decision-making processes as a leader?
7. What steps are taken to ensure that stewardship is not solely focused on fundraising and money management but also spiritual growth and discipleship?

Chapter Eight (Key Seven): Agape Love

Beyond being a great humanitarian, Derek's title of "Father" alone couldn't capture the essence of who he truly was. What it means to be more than just a father reflects Derek's true identity. His children were his world. Every decision he made was driven by one purpose: his kids. While many people might say, "I work for my kids" or "I stopped living recklessly for my kids," Derek took it further. For instance, not only did he monitor the cleanliness of his surroundings, but when he saw trash that did not originate from him, he picked it up, thinking, If my kids are watching, I want to set an example for them. Derek made sure his actions never reflected negativity or anything that might lead his children astray. His sole motive was their success, and he never wanted to be the reason they failed.

When it came to his children's future and their very right to live, Derek often said there was no limit to what he would do for them—even if it meant giving his life. As honorable as that declaration was, and though many parents say the same, few ever imagine they'll be asked to prove it. But for Derek, that day came.

Derek, a few mutual friends, and I were in his "man cave" watching a Mets game when a piercing wail rang out from the other side of the house. It was his wife. Their son had collapsed in the driveway and was unresponsive.

As we all ran outside, 911 was called. While we waited for EMS, one of the guys visiting administered CPR was administered. The paramedics arrived quickly, took over, managed to resuscitate him, and rushed him to the hospital.

His lungs had become toxic, affecting other organs throughout his body, including his heart, which led to it stopping and Derek Jr. collapsing.

His condition was described as "unexpected and previously unfounded," especially given his athletic lifestyle. He was a kid's kid: full of energy, always in motion, involved in multiple sports, and known for his playful nature. To his parents, this condition came out of nowhere.

Hours passed before a doctor finally came out from the back with news. Though Derek Jr. was stable, the doctor delivered the hard truth: Derek Jr. had an undiscovered condition with his lungs that caused his collapse, and a donor was needed immediately. Derek responded to the doctor's words. He asked, "What about me?"— meaning what about one of his lungs? Could he be tested, and if he was a match, could his lungs be used?

The doctor launched into a thorough explanation: the risks, the medical uncertainties, what could go right—and what could go terribly wrong. He explained that Derek might not survive the procedure, especially given him having a history of heart issues. In my opinion, the doctor was being fair, laying out every possibility. But Derek only saw one thing: his son's need.

"How fast can I be tested?" he asked.

The doctor replied, "Immediately."

The test showed Derek was a match. But the warnings were clear—this surgery could cost him his life. Still, he didn't waver.

He stressed to the doctors, to us, and to his wife that there were no limits to what he would do for his son, not even the limit of his own life.

After confirming his wishes and asking us, his friends, to be there for his family if things didn't go as hoped, the surgery was scheduled. Two days later, it happened.

Out of this series of events I witnessed, what struck me most was how Derek entered into this with complete resolve—no fear, no second thoughts. He was ready to give everything so his son might live. In all my years, I had never witnessed self-sacrifice at this level. I'd heard of love like that, read about it, maybe even prayed for it. But to *see* it—raw, real, and unfolding before my eyes—was something else entirely.

This was love without limits.

Love with no conditions.

Love given without expecting anything in return.

Derek's gift to his son reminded me of another sacrifice—the one made by Jesus, who gave His life so that we all might live, with no guarantee we'd ever love Him in return. Derek's only desire was to give his son a chance, and he believed that chance was worth everything he had.

He believed that chance was worth giving all of himself away.

That day, Derek expressed what few are willing to express to another: he extended to his son, Agape Love.

AGAPE LOVE DEFINED

Agape love is not easily defined. In many ways, it is not simply understood, especially when compared to how love is often portrayed in modern culture. What we see and believe love to be today can cloud our perception of *agape*. To truly grasp its meaning, we must return to its roots.

The term *agape* is derived from the Latin *agapē*, which originates from the Greek *agápē*, a word used to describe deep, committed, and selfless love often translated as brotherly love (Merriam-Webster, 2025). However, in this context, and in alignment with biblical usage, *agape* refers to the highest form of Christian love. It is a kind of love that moves beyond sentiment, it is action rooted in empathy and grace, expressed through a genuine desire for the well-being of others. It seeks the good of the beloved, offering help, demonstrating kindness, and giving of oneself with no expectation of return. *Agape* love is for everyone.

At its core, *agape* is sacrificial. It costs something. It is a love that reflects the grace of God, freely given and deeply felt (Symington & Symington, 2018). Returning to the Greek, *agape* reflects a love called out of one's heart by the value and preciousness of the one being loved—not because of merit, but because of intrinsic worth.

Writer John Van Wagoner offers a profound definition of *agape*:

"A love that values, esteems, respects, and honors another person because of their intrinsic value and worth. Agape love is not based on the other's behavior or attributes, such as beauty, wealth, possessions, or intelligence. It is not based on their accomplishments or performance, and it is not based on whether they like you or not.

Agape love arises from an act of God's will." (Van Wagoner, 2016) We often equate love with feelings or emotion, but Van Wagoner further emphasizes:

"There is no emotion involved in agape love, so feelings are not required to manifest it." (2016)

This makes *agape* distinct from other types of love. It is not born of attraction, chemistry, or obligation. It is love at its highest, purest level. It is love by choice—a conscious decision made not out of desire, but out of principle.

As Winston (2002) puts it:

"Agape love is a moral love, doing the right thing at the right time for the right reason. More specifically, *agapao* means to love in a social or moral sense, embracing the judgment and the deliberate assent of the will as a matter of principle, duty, and propriety, and embodies selflessness, sacrifice, and unconditional care for others."

This is the kind of love Derek showed. It wasn't driven by emotion, obligation, or recognition—it was an intentional offering, rooted in moral clarity and divine reflection. It was *agape* love in action.

True *agape* love is what defines the very identity of God. It's not sentimental or circumstantial—it flows from His essence. God loves not because of what we do, but because of who He is. His love is not conditional or reactive; it's a consistent outpouring of His unchanging nature.

For Bible readers throughout history, agape ideas clearly expressed continually by the life of Christ and for Bible readers throughout history, *agape* is the clearest expression of Christ. It's not just something He demonstrated—it's who He is. Today, *agape* love remains the calling and priority of every authentic Christian. It is central to the command Jesus gave to all who would follow Him.

The Greatest Commandment tells us to love God with all our heart, soul, mind, and strength—and to love our neighbor as ourselves. In this, Jesus calls us to replicate Him: to love as He loved.

As Christians, we acknowledge the immeasurable forgiveness we've been given. And the name—the identity—we've been blessed to receive should be the very thing we extend to others. That extension is a reflection of grace, because the forgiveness we've received wasn't earned. It was a gift—freely given, out of love.

This act of giving—especially when undeserved—is the essence of *agape*. Its love is rooted in empathy, in selfless kindness, in treating others not according to merit but according to mercy.

Though Christian's are called to care for all people in the name of Christ, the Bible makes this demand to follow very clear as God himself is the standard for true Agape love and animals authentic in their faith when with all their heart and edits, they follow the way of the Lord (Roat, 2024).

Agape love involves extending oneself as a Christian toward another. *Agape* means action. It cannot be represented without the giver bringing themselves—fully and intentionally—to the one receiving it. The giver of *agape* love offers it selflessly, expansively, and with deep intentionality, always for the benefit and vitality of the receiver.

Believers who extend *agape* love carry a felt sense of loving responsibility and devotion toward those they serve. While they may give much, they expect nothing in return (Fleming, 2024). This is the essence of unconditional love.

It is here that *agape* love and leadership intersect.

Christian leaders are called to constantly consider the needs of those they lead. This kind of leadership is expressed through service—empowering others by attending to their needs. It is not about authority or recognition, but about creating a supportive and collaborative environment where everyone is valued and able to thrive.

As Christ commanded, those who desire to follow Him must deny themselves. This call to self-denial defines the Christian leader. And from that place of humility and surrender, they become vessels through which God's *agape* love is shared with those they lead.

THE GOOD SAMARITAN

Stemming from a question posed to Jesus about eternal life, His response led to one of the most well-known parables in scripture—the story of the Good Samaritan. Whether seen referenced in a hospital name, charitable organization, or used to describe a selfless act, the title "Good Samaritan" is familiar to most people, especially Christians.

During His exchange with the attorney, Jesus could have answered with a theological explanation about the mechanics of salvation. Instead, He chose to illuminate a deeper truth: the importance of love expressed through action— particularly love extended toward those we might not naturally consider our own.

Through this parable, Jesus highlighted that love is not merely a concept, but a requirement. He emphasized comradery— not just among peers or those close to us, but toward anyone in need. The Samaritan's actions transcended cultural, social, and religious divisions. Jesus used this moment to make something profoundly clear: love is a determining factor in faithfulness to Him, and it is foundational to effective leadership.

The Parable of the Good Samaritan (Luke 10:25–37, NIV) tells of a man traveling from Jerusalem to Jericho who is attacked by robbers. They strip him of his clothing, beat him severely, and leave him lying on the road, half-dead.

Shortly after, Jesus describes how a priest comes along the road, sees the injured man—and intentionally crosses to the other side, avoiding him. Then a Levite approaches, sees the same man suffering, and also passes by without offering help. Finally, a third individual enters the scene—a Samaritan.

To Jesus' audience, this would have been shocking. Samaritans were regarded as a lower class by the Jewish people. Historically, they had intermarried with non-Jews and did not strictly observe the Law of Moses, leading many Jews to treat them with disdain, even to the point of religious and social excommunication. In their eyes, a Samaritan would be the *least* likely person to offer aid. And yet, it is the

Samaritan who stops. It is he who sees the injured man—not as a burden or threat, but as a human being in need. While the parable does not clarify whether the beaten man was a Jew or a Gentile, that detail is irrelevant to the Samaritan. His objective was not bound by culture, history, or social expectations. His aim was simply to help.

This is where the heart of the parable lies. The Samaritan chose to go beyond himself—beyond prejudice, beyond division, beyond fear—and render aid to someone vulnerable. His decision to engage was intentional, costly, and compassionate. He tended to the man's wounds, placed him on his own donkey, brought him to an inn, and paid for his continued care.

The critical lesson here lies in the Samaritan's *choice*—a choice to love through action, to demonstrate *agape* love when it was least expected, and most needed.

The Samaritan did not merely perform the basics. He went far beyond simply getting the injured man back on his feet or brushing the dust from his body. He tended to him with intentional care—disinfecting the man's wounds with wine and soothing them with oil to ease his pain. Then, lifting the man onto his own animal, the Samaritan gave up his own comfort, choosing to walk beside him. He took the man to an inn, ensuring he had a place to rest and recover.

But even then, he didn't stop.

The Samaritan paid the innkeeper with his own money and further promised, *"Take care of him, and when I return, I will reimburse you for any extra expense you may have."* His concern didn't end when the man was no longer in immediate danger—it extended to his full recovery. This wasn't just a gesture; it was a full, sacrificial commitment to another human being's well-being.

Jesus shared this parable in response to a question about eternal life. Rather than providing a theological breakdown of salvation, He used this story to dismantle cultural pride, religious bias, and the illusion of righteousness without compassion. The man who questioned Jesus - who likely contained indignation toward Samaritans - was being shown that true obedience to God cannot coexist with prejudice. Jesus was making it clear that cultural, religious, or social boundaries must never override the command to love.

This kind of love does not merely reflect social courtesy—it reflects the very heart of God.

The Good Samaritan is not just a moral example; he represents the standard God sets for His people. Believers are to lay down their biases and extend compassion to all, seeing *every person* as our neighbor. More specifically, our neighbor is anyone God places in our path.

This is our calling: to love all of humanity with the same selfless, boundless love that Jesus both demonstrated and commanded those following Him. This love is not passive—it is active, sacrificial, and faithful. It is *agape* in action.

Agape love, as demonstrated through Jesus' story of the Good Samaritan, is made unmistakably clear. This love is sacrificial—it centers not on self, but on the needs of others.

One of the most profound actions in the parable is that the Samaritan *stopped*. He interrupted his journey, put his own plans on hold, and responded to someone in need. That moment of stopping is crucial—not only in the story itself but in the greater message of *agape* love. Despite religious, cultural, or personal differences, and even knowing the injured man may not have done the same if roles were reversed, the Samaritan chose to see the injured man as his neighbor, not a stranger. And he stopped.

Then, he *gave*. He guided the broken man toward restoration, giving generously of his own resources—his oil, his wine, his animal, his time, and his money. He didn't just provide momentary relief. He made a commitment to this man's continued care.

Finally, he *vouched* for him. The Samaritan asked the innkeeper to continue caring for the man in his absence and promised to cover any future expenses. This was not just help, this epitomized the command of Christ to "love thy neighbor."

Agape love is a self-sacrificing love. As Winston (2002) states, it represents total commitment—even unto death. That means true love costs the giver. And this is the kind of love that Christian leaders are called to embody.

The Good Samaritan, though not an official leader, reflected the very characteristics and principles that define effective Christian leadership. R.C. Chapman rightly observes:

"Jesus calls leaders to sacrificially serve one another, to forgive when the opportunity presents itself, and to treat one another as brothers and sisters in the family of God." (Peterson, 1995)

In the same way, Christian leaders must prioritize the needs of others above their own. This is the essence of servant leadership through the lens of *agape* love. Compassion and selflessness should not be reserved for those already within the faith—but extended even to those considered outsiders or strangers.

True Christian leadership does not discriminate. It does not seek reward or recognition. It reflects the love of Christ to all people, regardless of their background or identity.

When *agape* love leads, hearts are revealed. Opportunities for kindness are seized. And in each act of compassion, Christ is made visible. In showing love, leaders expose Jesus to those who may desperately need Him—even if they do not yet know Him.

Ultimately, when leaders demonstrate *agape* love, they reflect the true nature of Christ. And through that reflection, they open the hearts of their followers to discover the fullness of His saving power, His grace, and His ability to restore what is broken in *all* of us.

WHY AGAPE LOVE IS IMPORTANT TO CHRISTIAN LEADERSHIP

The Greek word *Agape* describes a divine love that continually gives—even if it is never returned, acknowledged, or appreciated. It is a love that persists regardless of the response, rooted not in emotion or condition, but in value and intentionality. *Agape* love emerges when an individual sees, recognizes, and understands the intrinsic worth of a person or object. It stirs a love so profound that it knows no boundaries—no limits to how far, how wide, how high, or how deep it will go to be expressed.

It is a self-sacrificial love that propels the one who loves into action.

Clearly, *Agape* love is not something we can generate from our own human strength. As Renner (2025) explains, *Agape* is God's love. It is divine by origin and supernatural in function.

To put it simply: *Agape* is how God loves.

His love is without limit—unrestrained by condition or cost. God loves us without measuring the sacrifice it takes to love. He gives of Himself continually, whether that love is reciprocated or not. This kind of love doesn't retreat; it doesn't falter; and it does not fade in the face of rejection.

The Apostle Paul speaks of this love in his letter to the church in Ephesus:

"I pray that out of his glorious riches he may strengthen you with power through his Spirit in your inner being, so that Christ may dwell in your hearts through faith. And I pray that you, being rooted and established in love, may have power, together with all the Lord's holy people, to grasp how wide and long and high and deep is the love of Christ, and to know this love that surpasses knowledge— that you may be filled to the measure of all the fullness of God." *(Ephesians 3:16–19, NIV)*

Paul's words reveal that *Agape* love is more than theological knowledge—it's a reality to be *experienced*. It surpasses understanding and fills the believer with the fullness of God. And it is this love—this *Agape*—that must reside in the heart of every Christian leader.

Leaders called to the work of the Lord cannot lead in their own strength. They must lead from *within*, from a place where *Agape* love lives and thrives. It is only through this love that they can fully reach and minister to those whom God has entrusted to them.

Christian leadership that satisfies the Lord's heart must first be rooted in His love. For it is only when leaders are filled with *Agape* that they can exhort, shepherd, and serve others in a way that reflects the selfless heart of Christ.

Agape love is absolutely imperative for Christian leaders, as it mirrors the very actions of Jesus Himself. Paul emphasizes this in his letter to the Romans, stating, "God demonstrates his own love for us in this: While we were still sinners, Christ died for us" (Romans 5:8, NIV). For Christian leaders—whose mission is rooted in following Christ—this sacrificial love must be at the heart of their actions toward others.

Regardless of an individual's background, culture, intelligence, or past mistakes, *Agape* love transcends all boundaries. It reflects the true nature of Christ, who offers grace and forgiveness freely, without condition. As Christian leaders, our calling is to demonstrate that same love. We are called to go beyond personal comfort and boundaries to bless those in need. Our primary mission is to help others connect with the Savior—leading them to experience Christ's transformative power.

Just as Jesus Himself endured great sacrifice to save humanity, Christian leaders are called to do the same, even if it means taking on hardship or facing adversity. The goal of a Christian leader is not merely to lead but to guide others to Jesus— sometimes at great personal cost. It is through this self-sacrificial love that the lost come to understand the true nature of Christ, and it is this love that opens their hearts to follow Him. When we lead with *Agape* love, we invite others to walk alongside us as we walk with Christ.

The distribution of *Agape* love underscores the supremacy of God's love above all other forms of spirituality. When Christian leaders embody this love, they establish a template for those around them, creating a model that goes far beyond just leadership. While leaders are called to exemplify it, *Agape* love is meant to permeate all aspects of community life, fostering an environment of selflessness rather than selfishness (Roadcup, 2023).

Jesus demonstrated this powerfully in the Upper Room just before His crucifixion. In an act that would have shocked His disciples, Christ washed their feet—a task typically reserved for a servant or someone of lower social status. This moment of humility and service caused confusion among the disciples. They couldn't reconcile the image of their Teacher and Lord on His knees, performing a task so undignified by societal standards. Yet, Christ's actions were profound, and His explanation made clear the significance of His example: true greatness lies in serving others.

He said, *"You call me 'Teacher' and 'Lord,' and rightly so, for that is what I am. Now that I, your Lord and Teacher, have washed your feet, you also should wash one another's feet. I have set you an example that you should do as I have done for you. Very truly I tell you, no servant is greater than his master, nor is a messenger greater than the one who sent him. Now that you know these things, you will be blessed if you do them."* (John 13:13-17, NIV).

God calls Christian leaders to dedicate themselves fully to the care and preservation of His people. This is where *Agape* love deeply connects to leadership. Christian leaders must be both prepared and willing to go to the lowest and highest extremes in order to reveal Jesus to individuals and groups of followers (Bouch, 2024). *Agape* love requires leaders to care genuinely for others, embodying ethical behavior and setting a model for their followers.

This kind of love involves seeing followers as whole people—acknowledging their physical, mental, and spiritual needs (Carvalho & Mulla, 2020). Furthermore, *Agape* calls for self-sacrifice and impartiality, values demonstrated powerfully when Christ washed His disciples' feet. In this act, Jesus exemplified the humility and love that should characterize every Christian leader. Leaders are called not only to serve but to serve with selflessness, offering their time, resources, and compassion to those entrusted to their care.

Agape love is the seventh key, and for many, the most important, as it unites all the essential qualities required for effective Christian leadership. As the highest form of love that exists, *Agape* represents the love that God desires for every believer to embody.

Christian leaders must prioritize this love in their leadership approach, allowing it to define and manifest in their daily lives.

Agape love is not simply an emotion, but a "consciously chosen mindset that allows us to see others through a deep respect, grounded in a sense of oneness with them" (Carvalho & Mulla, 2020). This perspective enables leaders to respond to others as God desires—recognizing that His love extends to all, including sinners and those who, according to popular opinion, do not deserve love. As *Agape* love transforms the heart, it empowers leaders to offer grace—unmerited, undeserved, and unearned favor.

When Christian leaders live out *Agape* love, they extend grace relentlessly, drawing outsiders into God's fold and leading the lost to become followers of Christ. In doing so, *Agape* love transforms non-believers, revealing Christ to them in His true light. The consistent practice of *Agape* love by Christian leaders ensures the success of their calling, strengthens their discipleship, and creates a ripple effect where individuals are not only led to follow the leader but also to follow Christ. This transformation marks the true measure of effective leadership in God's Kingdom.

AGAPE LOVE APPLIED

C.S. Lewis describes *Agape* love as an active, selfless love that engages with an individual in thought, word, action, and deed, always working for the benefit of the other (Coe & Coe, 2007). When a Christian leader embraces *Agape* love, it creates an unexpected dynamic, one that transforms leadership practices. This is why, when *Agape* love defines a leader's approach and remains a central priority, its application becomes evident, even if its full impact is not always understood by others. Often, people notice that the leader interacts with others in a unique way, one that stands out from the norm. This is a reflection of Christ's ways, and as *Agape* love is applied, the outcomes often transcend the expectations of those around them.

Moreover, the results of applying *Agape* love bring multiple benefits—not only to the leader but also to their followers and the institution they serve. The transformative power of this love creates a culture of grace, empathy, and growth, which in turn fosters a thriving, unified environment for all involved.

When Christian Leaders apply the final key of Agape love to their leadership approach:

1. **Agape leaders continuously cater to their followers' needs.** Agape love is Spirit-driven, compelling Christian leaders to focus on the needs of those around them. When Agape becomes embedded in a leader's DNA, they actively seek out and meet the needs of their followers. Through the power and discernment given by the Holy Spirit, leaders move with a sense of purpose, guided by the example of Christ seen in GOD's Word. They are led to be in the right place at the right time, doing what God has called them to do. Agape love makes Christian leaders deeply sensitive to the needs of others, willing to be inconvenienced or interrupted when their help is needed. They are constantly ready to serve, putting the needs of their followers above their own comfort or convenience.

2. **Leaders functioning through Agape love do not discriminate.** Christian leaders who operate under Agape love do not judge others based on their background, history, or current condition. Instead, they respond to the needs of everyone, guided by the Holy Spirit, with the ultimate goal of leading others to Christ. Leaders filled with Agape love do not hold grudges or keep a record of wrongs. Their actions reflect the unconditional love they have for others, as they extend grace and share the message of God's love, regardless of the individual's past. They serve with the understanding that it is God's power

that can transform lives and bring restoration, and they are merely vessels of His love and mercy.

3. **Agape Love-driven leaders are givers who do not seek repayment.** Christian leaders are driven by the purest of motives, serving others without expecting anything in return. When Agape love is the foundation of their leadership, there is no sense of obligation placed on the follower; instead, leaders offer their love and care freely, without keeping a record or counting the cost. Too often, followers feel indebted to earthly leaders, but when a leader operates under Agape love, their focus is always on God. The leader's ultimate goal is to facilitate the reconciliation between God and the individual, not to seek personal gain or recognition. For leaders motivated by Agape, keeping track of their sacrifices or expecting repayment is far from their minds. What matters most is pleasing God, with no strings attached, and allowing God's love to flow through them to those they serve.

4. **Christian leaders defined by Agape Love will be noted for their compassion.** Compassion is the outward expression of Agape love, a practical demonstration that drives a leader's desire to serve others (Coe & Coe, 2007). Agape love challenges leaders to humble themselves, stepping beyond societal norms and the expectations of the institutions they represent. They allow themselves to be used in ways that may seem incomprehensible to some. Agape leaders are not afraid to get dirty and engage with the gritty realities of their followers' lives. They stand with those in need, reminding them that Christ is present even in their darkest moments. This genuine compassion, reflected in the leader's actions, not only helps those in immediate need but also inspires followers to rise up as

future leaders. Through selflessness, Agape love creates a ripple effect, drawing more people to the leader who demonstrates an authentic, empathetic understanding of their struggles and a deep desire to see them overcome.

5. **Agape love-purposed Christian leaders always prioritize God and His people.** Such leaders place their complete trust in the Word of God and the guidance of the Holy Spirit. This dependence prevents personal leadership agendas from interfering with God's will, positioning the leader as an intermediary between God's desires and the followers. This approach fosters trust between leaders and followers, establishing a firm foundation of truth. Even when the message is difficult to accept or contradicts personal emotions, the leader's responsibility is to deliver what God has commanded (Roadcup, 2023). By committing to God's correction, direction, and expectations, both the leader and their followers are called to align with God's will. In doing so, they experience His love in profound ways. Christ's words to the Jews in John 8:31-32 echo this principle: "If you hold to my teaching, you are really my disciples. Then you will know the truth, and the truth will set you free." (NIV). As Christian leaders, our mission is to prioritize the truth because it is through the truth that people find freedom. And when followers experience this freedom, as we follow the Lord, our leadership becomes truly effective.

SEVEN QUESTIONS TO ADVANCE THE UNDERSTANDING OF AGAPE LOVE FOR CHRISTIAN LEADERSHIP SUCCESS

1. How would you define Agape love?
2. Why do many hold the utilization of Agape love as a high priority for Christian leaders?
3. In what ways do you see Agape love impacting your leadership approach?
4. Besides the examples given, do you see Agape love extended in the Bible? If so, please describe.
5. If authentic Agape love is foreign in many Christian environments, please explain your belief as to why.
6. How can someone see God's Agape love in you? If so, in what ways?
7. Have you recognized someone in your life who extended Agape love to you? If so, please describe it.

THE CONCLUSION

Leadership is visible in every corner of life today. We see it in the brave individuals who wear police, fire, and ambulance uniforms, and in the members of the United States Military— whether Army, Navy, Air Force, Reserves, or Marines. Leadership is also found, though often overlooked, in our schools, from elementary to secondary levels, where teachers, administrators, and coaches play vital roles. Surprisingly, leadership is even seen in those whose roles are typically less acknowledged, such as janitors and cafeteria workers. Equally important, leadership should be recognized within the home, where parents, grandparents, and other family members influence and guide those in need of direction. Leadership is present in all aspects of life. However, while we see leadership in these various spheres, we also witness leaders whose influence does not have a positive impact on those they lead. Unfortunately, this creates a cycle where the next generation of leaders is left to grapple with ineffective leadership models, failing to display the qualities necessary for success.

This brings us to the Christian Church and the various organizations and institutions founded on Biblical and Christian theological principles. Historically, the Christian faith and the Church of Jesus Christ have played a pivotal role in shaping the standards of righteousness and guiding moral frameworks across the world. Though many may not realize it, if we examine our societies honestly, we see that the foundational principles for how we interact, live, and structure our communities have been deeply influenced by

Jesus and His teachings. This influence was not only vital for the followers of the faith but also for those called to lead these institutions. Christian leadership was seen as a way to help the world experience the profound truth and power of God's word through faith in Christ.

Sadly, if we are honest, we are witnessing a decline in the very principles and standards that Christ initiated. Instead of upholding His teachings, we are increasingly moving in the direction of the world, which the Bible cautions against, allowing the culture and values of society to guide the Church rather than the words of Jesus. The problem is that many leaders within the Christian faith and the institutions that bear Christ's name are failing to lead people toward Jesus. Instead, they are allowing secular culture to shape the direction of the Church, adopting ways that seem right to man, as Solomon warns in Proverbs 14:12. According to this biblical wisdom, such a path leads us toward a disastrous and irretrievable end.

Referring back to the central theme of this writing—Christian leadership—we must face a harsh reality: we are failing. While this does not apply to all leaders, as many have genuinely embraced the principles discussed here, the truth is that too many are falling short. To be specific, a significant number of Christian leaders are failing in their leadership duties and in the proper handling of their callings. These failures, once discreet, are no longer hidden. They are now widely known and felt. This is not just an issue in the United States, It extends globally within multiple new and established Christian organizations. What was once a rare occurrence—perhaps yearly or monthly—has now become, sadly, a daily reality. Christian leaders are frequently accused and proven illegitimate due to financial mismanagement, inappropriate sexual behavior, and serious character flaws, which cause them to, in ignorance, reflect Satan's practices instead of the image of God.

Moreover, many leaders are mismanaging their own lives and leadership responsibilities, leading to unhealthy imbalances, multiple resignations, and physical and emotional health issues. The situation has worsened over time because the Church, both at the administrative and clergy levels, has failed to make these disappointments a matter of serious concern. We have made excuses, misinterpreted scripture to justify overlooking issues, and failed to maintain ethical accountability. As a result, we have cocreated an environment in the Church that lacks the moral integrity seen in the early Christian community, as recorded in the Book of Acts, which was marked by its power and devotion to God.

The modern Church, in many ways, has crippled itself. Leadership has made essential principles non-priorities—things that were once vital during Jesus' time and in the early years of the Christian movement. We have shifted our focus toward worldly standards of accountability, rather than upholding the call to be the Church of Jesus Christ. True leadership, as exemplified by Christ, involved a deep care and commitment to God's people. But today, many leaders, whether out of ignorance or intentional compromise, are more concerned with satisfying cultural aspirations than with fulfilling the demands of the Great Commission.

What is especially tragic about this situation is that most leaders have inherited these practices and fail to recognize or see the damage they have caused and continue to cause. In many churches today, leaders are more like hosts of a

Christian-type experience than true shepherds called to lead individuals toward professing Christ as Lord. The reason for this shift is rooted in the way they were taught to approach leadership—focused more on cultural appeal and the desire for applause, rather than honoring the expectations of the Lord. Many leaders, driven by a motive for worldly success, are heading toward failure. Their focus on achieving success, often at the expense of their commitment to Christ's teachings, leads them down a path that aligns more with worldly ambitions than with the sacrifices Jesus calls His followers to make.

A Hard Reset

Leaders, if we are being honest, we must acknowledge that a hard reset is needed when it comes to our approach to Christian leadership. A hard reset, much like when we press that small, hidden button on the back of a device to restore it to its original manufacturer settings, is exactly what we need. But it's not the church itself that requires a reset—it's those of us involved in the church. However, we cannot direct our frustration toward the congregants and participants in Christian churches and institutions.

They are simply responding to what is asked of them or what they have been taught is right. The true reason for the ineffectiveness of the church today lies with too many ineffective leaders. If we return to the basics, we must start by embracing these "seven keys" and applying them as our foundational approach to leadership. When we, as leaders, learn how to wield these keys properly, I am confident that the difference will be immediately noticeable. The necessary improvements will reverberate through our churches and institutions, creating a positive shift within the Christian world.

Along with applying these keys, leaders must also focus on restructuring themselves as part of their development and leadership practice, ensuring they follow what Paul emphasized: "Follow my example, as I follow the example of Christ" (1 Cor. 11:1, NIV). Every key presented in this writing was perfectly demonstrated to us by Christ Himself throughout His earthly ministry. While numerous examples were given of how these keys should be used, it is important to remember that God has inspired each of us in the way we should go, and ultimately, all of this inspiration comes from our Lord. Jesus modeled these principles through His own leadership, providing us with a clear path to follow. In my opinion, He did this so that we would have no excuse for failure, but instead, every reason to succeed.

CHRIST: THE PERFECT EXAMPLE

Jesus came to save the world, and that is an undeniable fact. He also came to establish the way for us. In fact, He made it clear that He *is* the way (John 14:6, NIV). This way is the path to heaven, the way to a restored relationship with the Father, and the way to experience life—and life more abundantly. Furthermore, Jesus spent His three and a half years of ministry on earth establishing what believers are called to accomplish in the life we live today. Anything the Lord called us to achieve, Jesus demonstrated and provided to His disciples, showing them what was necessary for victory in these pursuits. This teaching is not only for the disciples but for all who are called to leadership, guiding them in how to effectively share the Gospel with the yearning hearts across the world.

FOLLOW HIS LEAD

Success for Christian leaders is not only possible despite the obstacles and modern challenges we face, but it is also essential. Our communities and Christian organizations need leaders—leaders who are not just filling roles but who are committed to revealing the truth about the world and, more importantly, the better truth about God. We need leaders who inspire their followers not only through words but through their actions, the lives they live, and their deep connection with God. We need leaders who are dedicated to creating more leaders, ensuring that the Kingdom of God continues to grow and expand. This can only happen when leaders approach leadership with the mindset of success, defined by effectiveness rather than failure.

Effective leaders make an impact, but not for their own sake. Their goal is not to have followers exalt them, but to lead others toward the one they follow, encouraging them to continue walking in the same path. The most successful leaders are those who prioritize the seven keys: prayer, faith, vision, integrity, wisdom, stewardship, and Agape love. When empowered by the Holy Spirit, these keys define a leader's identity and shape their approach to leadership, steering them toward success rather than failure.

Sadly, many leaders today fail to access these vital attributes. Some are unaware of their value, while others have been taught alternate methods of leadership that often result in challenges, ineffective outcomes, and difficulties in raising up new leaders. This leads to the very failures we aim to overcome. But for Christian leaders, implementing these seven keys in their leadership is not a distant dream. Though the examples you've encountered may not have fully demonstrated these principles, we have a perfect model to follow— Jesus Christ. His life and ministry showcase the power of these seven keys, and it is through His example that we are not only inspired to embrace them but also empowered to lead effectively in the way He calls us to.

Jesus is the perfect example of a leader. He understood how to humble Himself before His Father, setting a powerful example. Jesus never resisted offering love to those who followed Him, and as a leader, He knew that His actions would be replicated by future generations. What He modeled was not only necessary but essential for the development of effective leadership. This is why, when we observe the seven keys demonstrated by Jesus, their application in a Christian leader's life becomes easier to understand and embrace.

Did Jesus need the seven keys? No, He did not. Jesus is perfect because He is God. However, He did use the seven keys— not for Himself, but to demonstrate their value to the leaders He was establishing, and to show future generations their effectiveness.

Through His actions, He illustrated the benefits of these keys by utilizing them properly and with dedication.

For instance, we see in Scripture how Jesus relied on the power of prayer—one of the keys—before beginning His preaching mission in Galilee (Mark 1:35, NIV). As His ministry approached a time of great personal discomfort, He prayed to God, asking that the cup He was about to face be removed, but ultimately choosing to obey God's will over His own desires (Luke 22:42, NIV). This is also a clear example of the faith key in action: placing complete dependence on God, despite the challenges our senses may reveal.

After Jesus ascended to Heaven, His ministry and influence continued through His interactions with future leaders. A prime example is His outreach to Ananias regarding Saul, who would later become one of the most influential Christian leaders. In this instance, Jesus demonstrated the vision key for Christian leaders. When Jesus stopped Saul on the road to Damascus and redirected his mission, He also spoke to Ananias, giving him specific instructions regarding this man who had been a threat to Christians. When Ananias hesitated, trying to reason with Jesus, He responded with the following:

"Go! This man is my chosen instrument to carry my name before the Gentiles and their kings and before the people of Israel.

I will show him how much he must suffer for my name." (Acts 9:15- 16, NIV)

Here, Jesus demonstrated the vision key to Ananias, revealing His ability to see not only who Saul was in the present but also who he would become and the important calling he would fulfill in the Kingdom. This vision was something that Saul, later known as Paul, would come to possess and apply in his own leadership, particularly with Timothy and Titus.

If we return to the early days of Jesus' ministry, we see His use of the integrity key, particularly during his time of being tempted by Satan. In this moment of vulnerability,

Jesus wasn't merely tempted—He was attacked by the Devil. Despite this, Jesus effectively utilized the integrity key by standing firm and resisting Satan's temptations (Matt. 4:1-11, NIV). When Satan tried to offer Jesus what He needed or what He could have accepted in His time of need, Jesus remained steadfast, relying on God's Word and upholding the standards that defined His identity.

In John 8, the religious leaders approached Jesus, questioning how He would handle the consequences for a woman caught in the act of adultery. Jesus understood their true intentions. Their motive wasn't justice—it was to place Jesus in a compromising position and expose any perceived hypocrisy in His approach to Godliness. By publicly shaming the woman, they hoped to make themselves appear righteous, believing her death would validate their flawed understanding of the Law.

Jesus, however, used the wisdom key to perceive their hidden motives and turn the situation around. With remarkable insight, He allowed these self-righteous individuals to expose their hypocrisy publicly. When questioned about what should be done with the woman, Jesus responded, *"Let any one of you who is without sin be the first to throw a stone at her"* (John 8:7, NIV). His response revealed their inner sinfulness and caused them to walk away, as their desire to stone her was an act of self-righteousness that exposed their own sinful thoughts and actions.

Earlier, we discussed the importance of time in leadership, and no one exemplifies the wise use of time more than Jesus. With less than four years to accomplish the unimaginable—to fulfill the promise of Messiah and offer eternal life through His sacrifice— Jesus managed His time with great intentionality. Scripture shows Him as purposeful, saying, *"I must work the works of him that sent me, while it is day: the night cometh, when no man can work"* (John 9:4, NIV). Jesus knew that time was a limited resource, and He used it wisely, ensuring that He fulfilled His divine mission while honoring God as He modeled the stewardship key.

Finally, there is no greater example of Agape love than Jesus' sacrifice on the cross, where He gave His life for the sins of all humanity. Through His death, He provided believers with the way to experience a lifelong, relational connection with God (John 15:13, NIV).

We must also consider the beginning of Jesus' ministry, marked by His baptism. It was in this moment that He received the Holy Spirit, which would empower His leadership and human endeavors, making Him the most effective leader the world has ever known. At the same time, this event served as a powerful example for all future leaders, showing them what would be required to fulfill God's demands and to be effective in advancing His Kingdom (Luke 3:21-22, NIV).

YOU ARE CALLED TO BE AN EFFECTIVE CHRISTIAN LEADER!

Jesus demonstrated all of these keys through the power of the Holy Spirit. His mission and empowerment were intentional, serving as a template for future leaders—not merely to imitate Him, but to effectively fulfill God's calling. Leadership is the initial calling, but true success in leadership comes from faithfully carrying out God's will and achieving the purpose He sets before us.

For a Christian leader to be truly successful, they must follow the example Christ set. If Christ emphasized and utilized the seven keys, then their application is essential to a leader's approach. By embracing these keys, a leader can strengthen and refine their practices, ensuring their efforts are aligned with God's direction. If a leader finds themselves straying off course, the application of these keys can redirect their focus, ultimately leading to fruitful missions and the development of future leaders.

Moreover, the distractions and pitfalls that Satan brings—stemming from a lack of focus or the temptations of the world—can be mitigated by the strategic use of these keys. Through dedicated application, a leader can stay grounded in their mission, remaining steadfast in the faith.

For example, consider how regularly utilizing prayer—one of the gifts God has given—not only strengthens one's ministerial practices but also supports the minister themselves, ensuring their safekeeping and nurturing their heart. Reflect on the power of faith, which serves as a reminder of God's goodness and reassures leaders that He will continue to be faithful in all things, especially in their leadership roles.

Think about integrity, a quality many leaders lack, and the shortcomings that come with neglecting its importance. Integrity leaves a lasting impression on followers, especially the youth, who are keenly observant of the example set by their leaders. As leaders, we are accountable for what they see in us, and we have the responsibility to introduce them to the righteousness of Christ.

Without integrity, we fail in this most crucial task.

The Holy Spirit enables us to capture and step toward the vision God provides, allowing leaders to project that same vision to others. This empowers us to inspire excitement about the future and to recognize the significant impact people can make under our leadership. By anticipating the wisdom God will bestow, we find answers more regularly and ensure the success of the significant missions He has entrusted to us.

Our goal is not to be recognized as wise but to ensure that God is reflected through the decisions we make for His Kingdom. True care exists in stewardship, especially when a leader interacts with God's people, always remembering that they belong to Him. Sadly, this often goes unnoticed by leaders and is not always experienced by church congregants and members of Christian institutions. Stewardship teaches that leaders are not the owners; rather, they are entrusted with what God has placed in their care. Recognizing this responsibility fosters a desire to treat God's people with the utmost respect, understanding that the way we interact with them impacts the outcome and ultimately brings glory to God.

Finally, Agape love calls for leadership self-sacrifice, a necessary quality for Christian leaders. This sacrifice ensures that leaders are not only admired but also that love is exemplified within the community. Through this selflessness, followers can see a reflection of Christ in the leader, as God intended when He placed these leaders in their lives.

Overall, the seven keys are not a quick-fix solution on their own. It's important to remember that without the Holy Spirit, these keys—and we as leaders—will continue to function ineffectively. The keys connect us to the power that enables us to reflect Christ's approach to leadership. This writing serves as a helpful template, reminding us to apply what Christ demonstrated, while also teaching us to rely on the Holy Spirit—the friend who provides what we need to fulfill the success that God desires for us.

The Holy Spirit is our key chain, guiding, empowering, and continually endorsing our use of the keys He has given us, bringing together and holding together the blessings we possess, these tributes, principles, and tools, that ultimately guide and empower us to achieve the success God has positioned next to our names.

I believe that by doing so, we as leaders will experience growth, reaching higher levels of achievement and leading more individuals to faith in Christ through a Biblical approach. These keys are a guide, and when used properly, they lead us toward the blessings we wish to impart to our followers and enable us to make a lasting impact on the communities around us in the name of Christ. In the end, the seven keys serve to strengthen our leadership effectiveness.

Now, after engaging with this writing, I ask you: Are you ready today to be the leader you are called to be? Do you desire to see what resides in your heart regarding leadership success become your reality? Is your ultimate goal to please God, to reflect Christ in your walk, and contribute to the furthering of God's Kingdom?

If you've read this far, I believe your answer is yes. And with that, we must acknowledge this: we don't need ordinary leaders—we already have enough of those. You are called to be a leader of significance, a leader of strength, a leader who brings change, and a leader who builds. The Body of Christ needs leaders who are driven by a deep desire to enrich God's Kingdom. Whether in the professional world, the home, or in the church, your leadership is meant to impact those around you, and in turn, those you lead will become tomorrow's leaders.

Failure is not part of your future. You won't be your headline or a dark mark in the timeline of the other Christian leaders who fell short. Instead, God calls you to be the individual who achieves the very objectives He placed in your heart—the ones He created you to accomplish, and impact the many people he has placed around you. And within you, God has already provided everything necessary to make your success as a leader a reality.

To bring it all together, every leader needs a reminder of the essential principles, attributes, and tools that God has graciously given us. The seven keys are waiting for you—they will unlock the door to the success God has declared for your leadership. Through these keys that you have, success will not just be something you strive for, success will be how you are defined, and successful will be the way your leadership will be categorized. But remember, success is not viewed as such from a worldly perspective, but from a Kingdom perspective. That is why God's plan is for you to be successful, leading toward your time as His chosen leader to be **EFFECTIVE!** You are called to impact, influence, and leave a lasting impression, using the gifts God has given. The real question is, will you embrace them, and will you now confidently allow God to lead you toward the successful, effective leader you were born to be?

Allow God's Spirit to guide you in applying these seven keys, in every aspect of your leadership journey, and watch how **EFFECTIVE** you will become as a leader.

REFERENCES

Abel, K. M. (2011). Sources of adolescent Faith: Examining the origins of religious confidence.

Interdisciplinary Journal of Research on Religion, 4–5.

Ayers, M. (2021, January 4). The value of vision in leadership. For the Church. https://ftc.co/resource-library/blog-entries/the-valueof-vision-in-leadership/

Baker, B. (2023). Lessons from Joseph's stewardship. Book Baker. https://www.bookbaker.com/bn/v/Stewardship-The-parent-youare-Lessons-from-Josephs-Stewardship/8affa628-2f17-4ede-981148519f542bc7/6

Baptist Community Ministries. (2023). Top Christian leadership qualities that define a Christian Leader.

Breeze Church Management.

https://www.breezechms.com/blog/christian-leadershipqualities#:~:text=Personal%20wisdom%20in%20Christi an%20lea dership,at%20work%20in%20all%20circumstances

Barton, D., & D. D. (2022). Pastoral problems and reasons why.

Wallbuilders.

Barton, T., & TT. (1997). The Christian Leader As a Spirit Driven visionary. Asbury Theological Seminary.

Bechervaise, C. (2013, October 14). 5 reasons why vision is important in leadership. Tip.

https://takeitpersonelly.com/2013/10/14/5-reasons-why-visionisimportant-in-leadership/

Bishop, J., & McKaughan, D. J. (2023). Faith. Stanford Encyclopedia of Philosophy.

Blackaby, R. (2020, March 9). The wisdom needed for leadership.

Biblical Leadership. https://www.biblicalleadership.com/blogs/the-wisdom-needed-forleadership/

Blair, J. (2023, April 12). On Faith and Leadership. LinkedIn. https://www.linkedin.com/pulse/faith- leadership-jeff-blair/

Bouch, J. (2024, May 30). Understanding and applying agape love.

ForgeTruth.com. https://forgetruth.com/understanding-and-applying-agape-love/

Boxx, R. (2020, April 6). Lessons from A fellow named Bezalel.

CBMC International.

https://www.cbmcint.com/lessons-from-a-fellow-

namedbezalel/#:~:text=But%20God%20was%20not%20calling,ap pointe d%20to%20lead%20the%20way

Brodie, J. (2024, January 11). What is the fear of the lord?

Christianity.com.

https://www.christianity.com/wiki/god/what-is-the-fear-ofthelord.html

Brooks, N. (2017). AbrahamLincoln.org. The Gilder Lehrman Institute.

https://www.abrahamlincoln.org/features/speecheswritings/abraha m-lincoln-quotes/index.html Brown, J. O. (2014). The importance of Integrity in Christian leadership. Asbury Theological Seminary.

Buckland, C. (2012, April 11). Insights on power, character, and the ministry. Freedom to Lead

International. https://freedomtolead.net/insights-powercharacterministry/?gad_source=1&gclid=Cj0KCQ jwsoe5BhDiARI sAOXVoUtaQGQD6ZCHT5_I9OsTmSefrAr3usl2CxV2 RQYM92Z4kGPb XX1VugaAqAyEALw_wcB

Carvalho, F. K., & Mulla, Z. R. (2020). Power of love (AGAPE) in leadership: A theoretical model and research agenda. South Asian Journal of Management.

Chabot, H. (2023, September 28). Why is integrity important in leadership? Babson.

https://entrepreneurship.babson.edu/why-is-integrity-important-inleadership/#:~:text=Leaders%20who%20demonstrate%20integrity%20garner,become%20a%20successful%20entrepreneurial%20lea der

Clinton, R. J. (2012). The making of A leader. NavPress.

Coe, K., & Coe, A. (2007). Agape. International Journal of Servant Leadership, 2–19.

Cole, A. (2020). Encyclopedia of psychology and religion.

Costello, T. (2017, December 21). Why church leaders stop leading. Reach Right. https://reachrightstudios.com/blog/church-leaders-stopleading/?utm_source=google&utm_medium=paid&utm_campaign=21236750540&utm_content=&utm_term=&gadid=&gad_source=1&gclid=Cj0KCQiA_qG5BhDTARIsAA0UHSJKGWN5B_niSA29NzJWbTCUPzd4N0ReCfTwWUqQRC5EAd2ifShMIBMaAlB

Costello, T. (2023, November 23). Why church leadership matters now more than ever. Reach Right. https://reachrightstudios.com/blog/church-leadership/

Cross, T. L. (2007). The Cambridge Companion to Evangelical Theology. Cambridge University Press.

Cymbala, J. (2018). Fresh wind, fresh fire. Zondervan.

Dash, D. (2001, October 21). Sharing the vision. Dashhouse. https://www.dashhouse.com/20011021sharing-the-visionnehemiah-211-18-html/

Davis, J., & J. J. (2024). Is the Holy Spirit really a "person"—With a distinct personality? Themelios, 13–19.

Davis, S., & S. S. (2020, July 14). The true meaning of integrity. Crosswalk. https://www.crosswalk.com/faith/spiritual-life/integrity-theparentof-character.html

Demaria, L. (2020, September 6). Why all good leaders pray. Bright as the Sun.

https://www.laurademaria.com/blog/2020/9/6/latest-article-whyallgood-leaders-prayer

Davis, J., & J. J. (2024). Is the Holy Spirit really a "person"—With a distinct personality? Themelios, 13–19.

Dictionary.com. (2024). Prayer. Dictionary.com.

https://www.dictionary.com/browse/prayer

Earls, A. (2024a, January 24). Public trust of pastors hits new record low. Lifeway Research.

https://research.lifeway.com/2024/01/24/public-trust-ofpastorshits-new-record-low/

Earls, A. (2024b, April 10). Why are more pastors thinking about quitting? Lifeway Research.

https://research.lifeway.com/2024/04/10/why-are-morepastorsthinking-about-quitting/

Ebert, D. J. (2025). The wisdom of God. TGC.

https://www.thegospelcoalition.org/essay/the-wisdom-of-god/

Effron, L. (2019, December 20). The scandals that brought down the Bakers, once among US's most famous televangelists. ABC News. https://abcnews.go.com/US/scandals-brought-bakkers-uss-famoustelevangelists/story?id=60389342

Eruotor, O. G. (2022). Leadership with Integrity: An Imperative for Effective Pastoral Counselling.

Contemporary Issues cum Cultural Realities, 75–86.

Fapohunda, B. (2021). The role of personal integrity in soulwinning:

A systematic review of the theological literature. Evangelical Review, 1–18.

Ferguson, S. (2023, January 6). What is discernment? Ligonier. https://learn.ligonier.org/articles/discernment-thinking-godsthoughts

Finney, C. G. (1980). The promise of the spirit. Bethany House.

Fleming, L. (2024, March 8). Agape love: The art of loving unconditionally. Very Well Mine

https://www.verywellmind.com/agape-love-8580332#:~:text=First%20used%20in%20the%201600s, love%20o f%20man%20for%20God.%E2%80%9D

Frank, J. R. (2022). Stewardship as a lifestyle (pp. 1–3). Christian Leadership Alliance.

Graham, B. (1988a). The Holy Spirit. Thomas Nelson.

Graham, F., & F. R. (2020b). Evaluating critical dysfunction of leadership in the church: Motivating the Church to growth. Liberty University Scholars Crossing, 12–14.

Grandchamp, G. (2024, March 6). What is the purpose of prayer?

Christianity.com. https://www.christianity.com/wiki/prayer/what-is-the-purpose-ofprayer.html

Greenleaf, R. K. (2002). Servant leadership. Paulist Press.

Hallock, M. (2023, April 18). Are you leading by faith? Preach.

Love Publishing. https://www.preachleadlove.com/single-post/are-you-leading-byfaith

Harmon, M. (2022, May 27). What does faith mean? Grace Theological Seminary.

https://seminary.grace.edu/what-does-faith-mean/

Heaster, D. (2021). Bible lives, 1 The patriarchs: Abraham, Jacob, and Job. Aletheia Publications, 14–20.

Henson, J. D. (2018). The role of Biblical values in the development of the mission and vision of ethical organizations. Journal of Biblical Perspectives in Leadership, 186– 196.

Hinks, D. (2000). About Job's Integrity. Journal 33.

https://www.journal33.org/other/html/jobinteg.html

Holl, R. M. (1998). What is prayer? Complementary Health Practice Review, 4(2),109–114. https://doi.org/10.1177/153321019800400204

Huizing, R. (2011). Bringing Christ to the table of leadership:

Moving towards a theology of leadership.

Journal of Applied Christian Leadership, 64–65.

Hull, B. (2006). The complete book of discipleship. NavPress.

Jegede, D. O. (2023). Church Administration in Nigeria: Problems and Way Forward. AJRCS Global

Research Network.

Jeremiah, D. (2017, March 31). Turning point. Facebook. Facebook. https://www.facebook.com/drdavidjeremiah/posts/integrityiswhen-a-persons-words-actions- and-values-are-aligned-the-bestway-to/10155063363004534/

Kamer, J. (2018). Steward leadership and Paul. Journal of Biblical Perspectives in Leadership, 1–9.

Journal of Biblical Perspectives in Leadership.

Kang-Kul-Cho, P. (2014). The integrity of Job 1 and 42:11-17.

Catholic Biblical Quarterly, 239–248.

Karthikeyan, C. (2024). Integrating Biblical wisdom into experiential servant leadership education: A literature review.

International Journal of Research Culture Society, 2–5.

Kelleher, R. (2023, May 1). Why wise leaders seek counsel and embrace humility. Inspired Leadership. https://ronkelleher.com/532-why-wise-leaders-seek-counselandembrace-humility/

Kimball, S. W. (1977). Jesus, the perfect leader. Bright spot Byui.edu, 1–3.

Kinnaman, D. (2023, April 19). Excerpt: What pastors Wish They'd been prepared for. Barna Research. https://www.barna.com/research/pastors-better-prepared/

Kok, A. (2015, February 23). Five Effects of the Holy Spirit on Christian Leaders. Open the Bible. https://openthebible.org/article/five-effects-of-the-holy-spiritonchristian-leaders/

Krejcir, R. J. (2002). The character of wisdom. Schaeffer Institute of Church Leadership. http://www.churchleadership.org/apps/articles/default.asp?articleid=42550&columnid=Krejcir, R. J. (2006). The character of integrity. Church Leadership.org.

http://www.churchleadership.org/apps/articles/default.asp?articleid=42531

Kumi-Larbi, A. (2021). Living a life of integrity as a Christian.

COPHQ, 66–70.

Kuza. (2024, March 19). The role of the Holy Spirit in Christian leadership. Kuza. https://kuzaapp.com/the-role-of-the-holy-spirit-in-christianleadership/

Kwabena Asamoah-Gyadu, J. (2024). Be imitators of me as I am of Christ. Lausanne Movement, 2–3.

Larson, S. (2017, June 6). The importance of Christian leadership.

The University of Northwestern.

https://www.unwsp.edu/blog/the-importance-ofchristianleadership/#:~:text=As%20Christians%2C%20we%20carr y%20the ,other%20people's%20view%20of%20Jesus.

Latchaw, J. (2023, February 19). 80% of Pastor's Feeling Unqualified. LinkedIn.

https://www.linkedin.com/pulse/80-pastors-feelingunqualifiedjeremy-latchaw/

Leadership Ministries. (2023, August 1). What is Christian leadership? Leadership Ministries, Inc. https://leadmin.org/articlesarchive/what-is-christian-leadership

Lee, W. (2014). Lessons on prayer. Living Stream Ministry: https://www.ministrysamples.org/excerpts/THE-MEANINGOFPRAYER.HTML

Lewis, C. (1980). Mere Christianity. HarperCollins.

Ligonier. (2024). Prayer. Ligonier. https://learn.ligonier.org/guides/prayer

Limburg, J. (1987). Sevenfold structures in the book of Amos. Journal of Biblical Literature, 1–4.

Lomenick, B. (2013, June 3). Christians on leadership, calling and career. Barna Research. https://www.barna.com/research/christians-on-leadershipcallingand-career/

Luther, M. (2010, January 25). Martin Luther's definition of Faith. Ligonier. https://learn.ligonier.org/articles/martin-luthersdefinition-faith

MacArthur, J. (2005). The MacArthur bible commentary. Thomas Nelson.

MacDonald, W. (2016). Believer's bible commentary. Thomas Nelson.

Magnelli, F. (2020). When church leaders fail. Biblical Education, LLC.

Malphurs, A. (2003). Being Leaders. Baker Books.

Malphurs, A. (2016, July 20). What does it mean to be a Christian leader? The Lutheran Home Association. https://www.tlha.org/uncategorized/what-doesitmean-to-be-a-christian-leader/

Martin, T. (2019). Wielding the of prayer: The use of prayer in conflict. Obsculta, 14–16.

Mather, H. (2024). What does it mean to be a Christian steward?

Resource UMC.

https://www.resourceumc.org/en/content/what-does-it-mean-tobea-christian-steward

Mathew, T. K. (2017). Spirit-Led Ministry in the Twenty-First Century. WestBow Press.

McCallum, D. (2024). Vision and Christian leadership. Dwell. https://www.dwellcc.org/essays/vision- and-Christian-leadership

Menking, S. (2017). King Solomon: Wisdom for Modern Leaders.

Shimane-u.ac., 55-56.

Merriam-Webster. (2025). January. Agape. Merriam-Webster, 20. https://www.merriam-webster.com/dictionary/agape

Ministries, I.T. (Dirs.). (2020). A vision for believers [Motion picture].

Mohler, R. (2025). Leadership as stewardship, Part One. The Southern Baptist Theological Seminary.

Albert Mohler.

Moore, R. D. (1983). The integrity of Job. Catholic Biblical Quarterly, 19–32.

Mujuru, F. (2023, October 25). Christian Faith's transformative influence in leadership. Medium.

https://medium.com/@fitzgerald.mujuru/christianfaithstransformative-influence-in-leadership-69fc44892385#:~:text=In%20summary%2C%20faith%20significa ntly%20shapes,ethical%20decisions%2C%20and%20promotes%2 0inclusivity

Nichols, T. (2007). The Pastor's role in vision-based leadership.

Journal of Applied Christian Leadership.

Northouse, P. G. (2022). Leadership theory and practice. Sage Publications.

Noyes, P. (2024, May 14). Who is the Holy Spirit in the Bible?

Christianity Today.

https://www.christianity.com/wiki/holy-spirit/10-roles-of-theholyspirit-in-christian-life.html

Omoasegun, O. (2022). Understanding the Christian leadership.

Bible University of Canada.

Ottestad, M. (2023). Leading with integrity. Moleadership.

https://moleadershipcoaching.com/blog/leading-with-integrity

Peterson, R. (1995). Agape leadership. Lewis Publishers and Roth.

Petty, M. (2022). Future focused leadership. Future Focused.

Piper, J. (2024). Leaders in the church speaking and living God's word. Bethlehem Conference for Pastors. Sint Paul: Desiring God.

Platt, D. (2019, June 29). More important than life. Radical. https://radical.net/podcasts/pray-the- word/more-important-thanlife-daniel-610/

Pringle, P. (2016, February 2). The Reason why Faith is Essential to Leadership. Vision is the Gift of Faith in Action. https://www.linkedin.com/pulse/reason-why-faithessentialleadership-phil-pringle/

Rapp, C. (2021, March 18). What the bible says about work: Integrity in leadership. Stone Table. https://www.thestonetable.org/what-the-bible-says-aboutworkintegrity-in-leadership/

Redmond, D. (2017, December 22). Practical considerations of an active Faith. The Carolina Messenger.

Reiland, D. (2023, January 2). How do God's gifts affect your leadership? Outreach Magazine. https://outreachmagazine.com/features/73543-how-do-godsgiftsaffect-your-leadership.html

Renner, R. (2025). The agape love of god. Our Vision. https://renner.org/article/the-agape-love-of-god/

Rigney, J. (2022, March 20). Kneeling among lions learning to pray like Daniel. Desiring God. https://www.desiringgod.org/articles/kneeling-among-lions

Roadcup, D. (2023, November 1). Agape love in the life of an elder.

Christian Standard. https://christianstandard.com/2023/11/agape-love-in-the-life-of-anelder/

Roat, A. (2024, April 17). What is agape love? Christianity.com. https://www.christianity.com/wiki/christian-terms/what-doesagapelove-really-mean-in-the-bible.html

Rodecap, E. (2023, August 14). Why is vision casting crucial for church leadership and tips on casting a vision? Playlister. https://www.playlister.app/blog/why-visioncasting-is-crucial-forchurch-leadership-and-tips-on-casting-avision#:~:text=Church%20leadership%20revolves%20around%20 guiding,and%20a%20sense%20of%20purpose

Rodin, R. S. (2010). The steward leader. Journal of Applied Christian Leadership.

Rollins, T. (2020, January 1). What does the Bible say about Vision?

Bible Journaling Study. https://www.biblejournalingministries.com/what-does-thebiblesay-about-vision/

Romer, T., & Ruckl, J. (2009). The Torah in the New Testament.

Journal for the Study of the New Testament.

Sande, S. (2023, February 15). The foundation of wisdom. Heaven on Wheels. https://www.heavenonwheels.org/p/the-foundation-of-wisdom Sloan, R. B. (2010). A Biblical model of leadership. In D. S.

Dockery (Ed.), Christian Leadership

Essentials (p. 480). B&H Academic.

Sproul, R. (2014). The Holy Spirit (pp. 3–26). Ligonier Ministries.

Sproul, R. (2023, September 29). What is Biblical stewardship? Ligonier. https://learn.ligonier.org/articles/what-biblicalstewardship Ministry brands. (2024). Stewardship in the Bible:

Teachings, examples and principles. Ministry Brands.

https://www.ministrybrands.com/churchmanagement/stewardshipin-the-bible Strange, J. (2023). How does the Holy Spirit speak to us? Bible Study Headquarters.

https://www.biblestudyheadquarters.com/blog/how-does-theholyspirit-speak-to-us

Strongs. (1798). Strong's concise concordance & Vine's concise dictionary of the Bible. Thomas Nelson.

Sundar, J., & Samuel, A. (2022). St. Paul's discourse and dialogue with King Agrippa and Governor Festus as a model for contemporary interreligious understanding and communication. Tattva–journal of philosophy.

Symington, M., & Symington, S. (2018, October 11). Understanding 'Agape Love' as the highest form of intimacy. Relate Strong.

https://boonecenter.pepperdine.edu/blog/posts/understandingagape-love.htm

Taketa, C. (2011, August 11). Why prayer is essential in the life of a leader. Lifeway. https://www.lifeway.com/en/articles/why-prayer-is-essential-forleaders

Tamas, I. (2017). Theological definitions of the word believe/Faith.

Sciences of Communications.

Thomson, M. K. (2017). Spirit-led ministry in the twenty-first century. WestBow Press.

Turner, J. F. (2021, July 1). Joseph, the faithful steward. LinkedIn. https://www.linkedin.com/pulse/joseph-faithful-steward-jill-foleyturner/

Tweedt, C. (2019). Faith and Philosophy. Christopher Newport University.

Van Wagoner, J. (2016). God is love—Agape love. Jesus Restores, https://www.jesusrestores.com/blog/part-1-god-is-love-agape-love Vanourek, G. (2022, August 9). Why leaders should create a culture of stewardship. Triple Crown

Leadership. https://triplecrownleadership.com/cultureofstewardship/

Wainaina, C. (2023). The clergy is failing in Kenya. The Standard.

Warden, J. (2023, April 1). Importance of prayer in leadership.

Reconcile World.

https://reconciledworld.org/flourish/importance-of-prayer-inleadership/#:~:text=As%20leaders%2C%20prayer%20is%20the,%3A%20Romans%2015%3A5%2D6

Watson, B. (2024a). Leading with the Holy Spirit. Lifeway. https://leadership.lifeway.com/2016/05/11/leading-with-the-holyspirit/

Watson, C. (2024b). What is Biblical stewardship? Christian Stewardship Network. https://www.christianstewardshipnetwork.com/blog/whatisbiblical-stewardship

Wengler, T. (2021). Reflection and prayer in leadership – A reflective examination. Academia.

White, J. E. (2009). Leading with integrity. Christian Leadership Alliance. https://ym.christianleadershipalliance.org/page/leadingwithintegriy

Wilkin, B. (2023, April 17). Did Daniel try to impress with his praying. GES. https://faithalone.org/blog/did-daniel-try-toimpress-with-hispraying-daniel-610-12/

Williams, K. (2021). Church leadership and prayer: Leading the way for Leaders to pray. Regent

University.

Wilson, J. (1994). Undergirding the effort with prayer. International Journal of Frontier Missions.

Winston, B. E. (2002). Be a leader for God's sake. School of Leadership Studies.

Winston, B. E. (2018). The Four C's of Christian leadership. Inner resources for Leaders.

Winston, B. E., & Patterson, K. (2006). An integrative definition of leadership. IJLS.

WOL Ministries. (2022). Can we grow in Faith? WOLM.

https://wolm.org/blog-post/becoming-closer-to-god?gad_source=1&gclid=Cj0KCQiA1Km7BhC9ARIsAFZfEItak

M0HRTFVpOzvYdo39lh_H0k_mCg4rJQu5wA7rUTbX1Rgk26y5 5caApGeEALw_wcB

York, J. (2003). The Lord will provide. Genesis 22.1–19. Leaven Pepperdine University.

Zylstra, S. E. (2019, May 14). (2024). Why Christianity quit growing in Korea. TGC International

Mission News. Prayer.

https://www.thegospelcoalition.org/article/christianityquitgrowing-korea/Dictionary.com. Dictionary.com.

https://www.dictionary.com/browse/prayer

BIOGRAPHY

Arthor L. Faber is an Oral Roberts University graduate with a master's in Christian ministry. He is the founder and proprietor of Telos Christian Life and Leadership Coaching, where the organization specializes in assisting the future development and formation of the leaders of tomorrow in established and grassroots corporations, helping innovative people launch new businesses with a Christian foundation and influence. Previously, he was the founder and chief executive officer of Platinum Business Enterprises in Long Island, New York, leading the company in offering over 500,00 natives within the region in urban hair care and beauty supplies since 1997. Mr. Faber is currently the founder and Pastor of Restoration Christian Fellowship Church in Aquebogue, NY, serving since 2014. Any inquiries or assistance toward your goals are welcome, as the way to make better Christian leaders and businesspeople for the future is to share what was once shared with us.

Telos Christian Life and Leadership Coaching

Arthor L. Faber

631 302 5650

PastorArt@MyRCF.org

ABOUT THE AUTHOR

Dr. Arthor L. Faber is a pastor, leadership and life coach, radio host, and entrepreneur, dedicated to sharing the message of Jesus Christ and preparing Christian leaders for future generations. With a deep love for the Holy Scriptures, Dr. Art has committed his life to empowering others with the foundational truths found in God's Word, believing it should be the defining factor in the lives of believers.

As a highly sought-after speaker and consultant, Dr. Art frequently shares his incredible life journey at conferences, workshops, and grassroots Christian organizations and churches. His story began in a local Baptist church, transitioned into his career as a celebrity DJ, and went through an intense period of spiritual transformation. This journey has led him to become one of today's most prolific voices and advocates for the Christian faith, inspiring individuals who seek to follow God wholeheartedly.

Dr. Art is a devoted husband to Nicole and a father to six adult children, as well as a proud grandfather. His prayer is that he leaves a lasting impression on his family and everyone he encounters, helping them to see the goodness of God, not just through his words, but also through his desire to serve Jesus. His overarching goal is to "die daily" for the sake of Christ, culminating in the hope of hearing from the Lord, "Well done, my good and faithful servant."

Connect with Dr. Arthor L. Faber

Web: ArthorLFaber.com

Web: Teloscoaching.org

Web: MyRCF.org

Facebook: PastorArtFaber

Instagram: https://www.instagram.com/arthorlfaber

SubStack: https://substack.com/@drarthorlfaber

LinkedIn: https://www.linkedin.com/in/drarthorlfaber

ACKNOWLEDGEMENTS

I want to convey my heartfelt appreciation, primarily to my Lord and Savior, Jesus Christ. It is by His grace that I have attained salvation, and He has led me to my present position, not for my own glory, but entirely for His.

I am deeply thankful to my wife, Nicole, who has made countless sacrifices throughout our marriage to enable God to work through me. I feel incredibly blessed to have witnessed God's presence in your life as well. The Lord has given me a life partner, and in you, I have found a true blessing, a treasure, and authentic love. I will always see you as more than just a wife and a friend; you represent the love that God has shown me. I pray for God's blessings and favor to be upon you forever.

To my mother, Karen, and my grandmother, Virginia, who are no longer with us but are now worshipping and praising Jesus in His heavenly home, your steadfast devotion and sacrifices for me have greatly influenced my heart, especially in my relationship with my father. I hope that the investment you made in me brings you pride.

To my children, I thank God for your lives every day, and I pray that what He has achieved through me is just the beginning of His grand plans for you. I am extremely proud of each of you and hope that, with God in your hearts, you will come to understand that our Lord can do far more than we can ask or imagine, in accordance with His power that is at work within us (Eph. 3:20).

Finally, to those who have accompanied me on this journey by supporting Effective! May God bless you. I pray that the Lord's love continues to light your path and direct your steps. I appreciate your faith in what God has placed in my heart, and I hope that, God willing, we can embark on another journey together in the future.

I love you all and please…
Pardon any errors.
Because of His grace, always,
Dr. Arthor L. Faber

www.ingramcontent.com/pod-product-compliance
Lightning Source LLC
Chambersburg PA
CBHW060947050426
42337CB00052B/1626